TOMORROW, TODAY

TOMORROW, TODAY

Colin Farquhar

ATHENA PRESS
LONDON

TOMORROW, TODAY

ISBN 10-digit: 1 84748 096 9
ISBN 13-digit: 978 1 84748 096 5

First Published 2007 by
ATHENA PRESS
Queen's House, 2 Holly Road
Twickenham TW1 4EG
United Kingdom

Printed for Athena Press

Contents

I.i Saturn Five, the Beginning 1980–1988

I.ii 1988–1991

I.iii 1991–1996

I.iv 1996–1998

I.v 1998–1999

I.vi The New Millennium, 1999–2000

I.vii 2000–2002

I.viii The Living End, 2003

I.ix 2004

I.x Top of the World, 2004

II.i Moving On… 2005

II.ii Come Together, 2005

II.iii To the Devil a Daughter, 2005

II.iv July 2005

II.v August 2005

II.vi August–September 2005

II.vii New Direction, 2005

II.viii October–November 2005

II.ix If Not Now? 2005

II.x It's Not The End, 2005

III.i End of Book Two, 2006

III.ii Flogging a Dead Horse, 2006

III.iii The Disease, Spring 2006

III.iv Put the kettle on… 2006

III.v Back on the Chain Gang, 2006

III.vi Size of a Cow, 2006

III.vii My Way... 2006

III.viii Kingdom Come, 2006

III.ix Walking Forward… 2006

III.x Regardless, 2006

I

I.i

Saturn Five, the Beginning, 1980–1989

Saturn Five

My baby took me on a trip last night.
We shot past the moon at 105
Spinning through the stars
Enjoying the ride!
We looped the loop round Saturn Five
Heading for the sun
With something on my mind
We hit the earth!
Oohhh
It was out of sight.
Good job I was wearing a seat belt!

1980

The Mirror

What do you see?
Where do you see it?
Have you seen me?
I see you!
Look in the mirror,
Is he really there?
She's there!
How can I identify with someone I don't even know?
What do you see?
Where do you see it?
Have you seen me?
I see you!
Look in the mirror,

Is he really there?
She's there!
I don't even have a photo of the bastard
Who left all those years ago
And left my mother in the lurch.
What do you see?
Where do you see it?
Have you seen me?
I see you!
Look in the mirror,
Is he really there?
She's there!
My mother is there!!!

1980

Love Is

Love is like a flower.
A seed in the wind
Finds a piece of ground,
Grows and grows.
Love is like flower.
A bud, a bud grows
and the flower turns into something beautiful.
Love is beautiful,
Love is like a flower,
Love is best.
Make love not war.
Making love is like a nuclear explosion
But once the love has gone
It's like an empty world.
Everybody is a stranger
Until love comes again.
Love is best.
Make love not war –
But you'll always love the one you lost
If you loved them at all.

1984

Let's Have the Night

No more room. Go away!
Leave me alone ahhh…
Share my room, it's really very nice!
Come on love, let's have the night,
Spin through the stars,
I don't care, maybe tomorrow.
Come on girl, let's have the night.
You are doomed!
You just can't win with old values.
Look around!
Look inside!
Look ahead!
Look high!
Cry, blow crying!
Disappear up your own,
Stay out, this one's mine.
Somebody's been talking
Talking for me!
No more, I've found myself.
Go away.
No more room. Go away!
Leave me alone ahhh…
Share my room, it's really very nice.
Come on love, let's have the night,
Spin through the stars,
I don't care, maybe tomorrow.
Come on girl, let's have the night.

1984

Got Ill

I went to college,
Art College.
Had a great time!
No worries, no cares,
Laughed with the boys.

I got a pass grade,
I was pretty good.
I got a job, a great job!
Went for more money
Got a new job, a useless job!
I lost my job,
Signed on for weeks and weeks.
Got ill.
Got put in hospital.
Got drugs and more drugs.
I got well.
Lost my confidence in art.
Had a job!
Lost my job.
Signed on for weeks.
I'm still signing on…

1984

St Crispin's

Help!
The men from St Crispin's
Are after me!
Hide me.
Hide me anywhere!
Dustbin, attic, boot of ya' car.
Don't let them fill me with any more drugs,
I'm so doped up!
Friday comes after Sunday,
Help!
The men from St Crispin's
Are after me!
Hide me, hide me anywhere
Drugs drugs drugs!!!
I like feeling indestructible,
Don't let them take it away.
It's always the same,
Taking the fun out of it,
The fun of being mad!
Lyrics are fun!

Lyrics are scary,
When you're loony, songs mean more!
Hide me!
Hide me anywhere!
The men from St Crispin's
Are after me...

1984

The Dawn of the New Tomorrow

I walk in fields,
Fields without fences,
Meeting new people!
Sharing the fruits of a dying planet.
No fears, no trouble,
Fields without fences,
Seeing far-off places,
Places we only imagine.
Heaven knows this is the time,
The time to share!
Believing in yourself
Is just the beginning,
Help the blind
To share the profits of an empty world!
No fears, no trouble,
Leading the life, the life
You only dreamt about...
Don't give us that crap!!!
The crap you put in our minds.
Dreaming is not for me, I want to live,
Live the life I want!
Money, love, food,
The best in life, life for all
Fix my motor!
Don't need your new shiny one
Use this land, don't exploit it!!!
Dreaming is not for me, I want to live,
Live the life I want!
Money, love, food,
Music for the young!

Keep it, save it,
Open your eyes.
Use this land, use this land
For the future,
The dawn of the new tomorrow,
We walk in fields
Fields without fences…

1984

My Eyes

My eyes,
My eyes are so large!
They see nothing,
Nothing that is not to be seen,
Open your eyes,
See what I see,
It's not so hard.
Religion?
God knows I'm a believer!
I don't need your book
With its colourful stories
And pretty pictures.
Your book wasn't written so long ago!
Expand your mind,
Let them in,
Heaven or hell, you decide!
Nobody left?
No heaven or hell.
My eyes,
My eyes are so large!
They see nothing,
Nothing that is not to be seen.
Open your eyes,
See what I see.

1984

The Night

The night comes
And I'm here all alone.
I look at my posters,
I look outside,
It's dark, very dark.
A star shines.
I wonder where the star is,
Is it in heaven?
Are we in heaven?
Who knows?
The night comes
And I cannot sleep.
I write a poem.
You read my poems.
Do you like them?
Am I wasting my time?
The night comes
And you read,
Read what I wrote last night.

1985

My Record Player

I have a hi-fi;
I don't know what it's worth,
But it cost me £600
And that was in 1979.
I've been collecting records
All my life;
Records like fifties Rockabilly
Echo and the Bunnymen
And Bryan Ferry.
I enjoy listening to music!
It's amazing how every tune is different!
I only recently got into David Bowie
Yet he's been going for years!

Have you heard of Ray Campi?
He's good!
I have a record player;
I enjoy listening to music.

1985

London by Coach

The door slides open with a hiss.
A man struggles with his case.
My foot rests on the first step
As a lady with her child
Pays her fare.
I step up,
Ask the driver for a return ticket.
As I walk up the coach
I look for a seat.
There are plenty.
I look for a seat that will make me
feel comfortable in order with
the others on the coach.
We pass through villages,
Some nice scenery.
We hit the motorway
And off we go!!!
We arrive!
The door slides open with a hiss
And my feet hit the streets of London!!

1985

Some Friends

I have a friend!
I met her in Leicester.
She has a friend –
I have two friends!
I gave them a lift home,
I had a car, an old car
We went places: discos, gigs,

Spear of Destiny, Cramps, King Kurt.
I have two great friends.
One of them cuts my hair,
She cuts lots of people's hair!
She has lots of friends.
My motor was scrapped!!
One or two people I know
Didn't come round any more.
My two friends whom I met in Leicester
Are still my friends.
Some friends take you for what you are…

1985

Drink

I've just got back from the pub!
I've had one too many,
My body is numb,
My head is swaying,
My feet are aching
From my new shoes
Which need wearing in.
I can't be bothered
With work tomorrow!
It's summer, time 11.30 p.m.
The window is open,
I'm sweating.
I've had one too many,
My body is numb.
Drink drink drink!!!
Why do I drink?

1985

Teddy on the CP Van

Teddy, teddy,
Why do you look so sad?
With the stuffing falling from your legs.

The kids liked you.
The council man said
Take him off!!
Teddy, teddy,
Why do you look so sad?
You were so happy
On the front of our van.
Now you're in with us.
Teddy, teddy,
Please be happy!
Happy for us.

1986

James Dean

Have you seen the film?
The film with some of his story?
I can associate with it!
Everybody is the same.
I had a job,
A job in a drawing office.
They're no different
From people in a factory,
President Reagan
Is just a man.
I could have tea with him,
Or anybody famous.
James Dean made it clear.
Have you seen the film?
I can associate with it!
You can do anything,
Go anywhere!
Be a James Dean…

1986

Smile

About five years ago
People hadn't heard of psychobilly-music.
It's now known as Trash!

And lots of people know of it.
I can remember playing the Cramps
To some girls,
It was in this girl's house.
Her friends smiled
And said
Rock 'n' roll! Bop bop boogie!
These days everybody's
Bop boppin' to the Cramps!
And I smile
Only smile!

1986

Quite Deep

I don't have many friends.
I find it hard to make friends.
You see I give the appearance of being childish,
But once you know me
I'm quite deep;
The childishness is a cover.
Alan –
That's the bloke in the record shop –
He's a friend!
I've been buying records in Corby
About four years now.
I know some girls in Boots –
They always stop and have a chat.
I met them through an ex-girlfriend.
I find it hard to make friends.
You see I'm quite childish,
But once you know me
I'm quite deep.

1986

A Hit Single

I had a hit single,
I was number one
For five weeks!

It's fun being at the top –
All that money as well,
My song?
You must have bought it!
It was about two years ago.
I've spent all the money now,
And I live with my parents.
I had a hit single,
I was number one.
You must have bought it!!

1986

Dawn Wasn't There

I went to a party!
A party in Stevenage.
It was Jenny's 18th.
I met some old friends,
Mostly girls;
I made some new friends.
I got drunk!
I got drunk because
Dawn wasn't there.
Dawn was an ex-girlfriend;
I was in love with Dawn.
I only went
Because I wanted to see her.
But she wasn't there!

1986

Teddy Boy

I'm a Teddy boy!
A Ted in the eighties,
Not the fifties.
I'm into Sigue Sigue Sputnik,
Not Elvis!
I'm a Teddy boy!
A Ted in the eighties.

I mix with Punks and Skinheads,
Not Teddy girls or rockers.
I'm a Ted,
A Ted in the eighties.
I like eighties rock 'n' roll.
Music's so much better than it used to be!!!
Tear it up bop bop!!
Smash it up bop bop!!
I'm a Ted,
A Ted in the eighties,
Yeah!!

1986

Lost Ourselves

Me and my girl
Lost ourselves last night!
We flew through the sky,
Over the hills
And through the valleys,
Over the clouds
Looking down on the earth.
In an ecstasy of love
We hit a whirlwind
And off we go!
Into the stars.
We fall to earth
And caress each other
Under the blazing sun.
Me and my girl
Lost ourselves

1986

Something Special

I knew a girl,
I loved this girl,
She loved me,
I was up!
She was down.

We had something special!
But because she was down
And I was up,
We lost what we had.
If only we could have met in the middle?
I knew a girl,
I loved this girl.

1986

God the Creator!

I am God the Creator!
Everything around me is in my imagination;
You are part of that imagination!
This poem is part of your imagination.
I am God the Creator!
The sun is part of my imagination;
If nobody imagined the sun,
The sun would not be there
And we would die!
You are God the Creator!
I am part of your imagination.
Who imagined us in the first place?
God the Creator!!!

1986

Corby Town

This town,
This town is so dirty
With its dual carriageways
Leading nowhere.
Houses upon houses
Filled with unemployed;
A sign saying Wonder World!
Just a sign.
Once a prosperous town,
The steelworks
Filling the sky with smoke.

Dirty town;
This town,
Four night spots
Filled with underaged drinkers,
Underaged drinkers
With no future.
This town;
No town.
Do you live in a town like this town?
Any town!!!

1986

Time!

Tick tock tick tock,
Time is strict,
Time is slow,
Time is fast,
Time has no emotion.
The clock on the wall,
Tick tock tick tock,
Ticks away,
Second by second,
Minute by minute,
Hour by hour.
Time to get up,
Time to go to bed.
Goodnight!!!

1986

Corby Town

Tear It Up!

I knew a man, a man in a band!
I bought some records from this man
And the man sang!
Tear it up, bop bop!!
Step back baby, move my way, come
    a little closer let me hear you
    say Tear it up, bop bop!!
This man sang like no other man!
The man in the band
Who sang
Tear it up, bop bop,
Tear it up, bop bop.
This man had a guitar,
A guitar, which every man's had
And now I've got this man's guitar.
The man who sang
Tear it up, bop bop!!

1986

Television

I don't watch much television.
Television can pollute your mind,
Television is someone's point of view.
The news is different all over the world;
On the same piece of news
Different people's point of view.
I don't watch much telly
Television can pollute your mind!!

1986

Television

King Kurt

We're off to London again!
To the Tropical Palace.
We ask a policeman the way:
Just down the road.
We park outside the doors.
Inside the Pogues are playing –
I thought the Pogues were good!
Ten minutes before King Kurt comes on
The plastic beer glasses start flying.
The hall is filled with beer glasses
Flying through the air.
King Kurt comes on!
The flour and porridge
Starts flying.
Everybody's covered
Including my motor!
I wondered why nobody had parked
Next to the doors!!
Lynda and I are waiting to go.
Carrie said she was going to a party.
An ambulance stops us from leaving
Carrie comes out half an hour later!
Are we ready to go???

1986

Brockwell Park

We're off to London!
We're going in my motor.
My car is old
But it should do it.
I've a car-full:
Lynda, Carrie, Simon and his girlfriend –
£5 each petrol!
I'm laughing.
Simon and his girlfriend
Spend most of the day in the car!

Kissing.
Lynda, Carrie and me
Go off to see the bands.
The GLC is footing the bill –
Don't we know it.
Communist flyers shoved in our hands.
They make good umbrellas –
It's raining all day.
God likes the GLC, hee hee!!
We see the Fall, Strawberry Switchblade
And many more!
I can't remember them all.
The Damned come on
With Captain Sensible!
Anyway, time to go.
Where are Lynda and Carrie?
Lynda finds the car sometime later.
Carrie, where's Carrie?
We go!!!

1986

Margaret

I've been here for eternity!
Top of the Pops ends this week,
Hell hell hell!!! Eternity.
Margaret The Boss smiles;
She's got to know?
Got to know!
Tell tell tell!!!
Eternity in the Box!
Full of drugs!
Hate drugs!
You're dead,
Living dead.
She knows!
Top of the Pops ends this week
I've been here for eternity!
Margaret didn't know!
But she knows now…

1988

Smoke

The fire has been burning
Since the dawn of time!
The smoke is getting thicker
With TV and radio,
News, gossip and propaganda
Flying around the world.
The fire has been burning
Since the dawn of time!
Do we see the fire
Or only the smoke,
The smoke governments let us see?
The smoke is getting thicker.
Let the light shine through
To help the world
Come to the New Tomorrow
Before the fire engulfs us all!
The fire has been burning
Since the dawn of time!
The smoke is getting thicker…

1988

Silent Children

Silent children
See it all,
Hear it all,
But still they are silent;
Silent children.
Please silent children,
Say hello to me!
No way out,
No way in.
Don't go, please stay.
No way out,
No way in.
Silent children.

4 March 1988

Up and Down

Up and down,
Up and down,
Up and down,
Still he walks.
Up and down,
In anticipation.
Up and down,
Up and down,
The sun wakes you up,
The moon puts you to sleep.
Day and night,
Day and night,
The sun wakes you up,
The moon puts you to sleep.
Up and down,
In anticipation.
Up and down,
Up and down,
Still he walks,
Up and down.

4 March 1988

My Cell

One in my cell today,
Two in my cell tonight,
Three in my cell tomorrow.
My cell is big,
My cell is small.
Please share my cell with me!
One in my cell today,
Two in my cell tonight,
Three in my cell tomorrow.

4 March 1988

UFO

From the skies they come,
To the skies they go.
Please say hello to me!
Say hello tonight
UFO
UFO
UFO
Hello UFO.
Please bring some food
For my family
UFO
UFO
UFO
Goodbye UFO.
Hello…

4 March 1988

The Big Boy's Toy!

Let me out,
Let me out,
With my new toy.
I like toys,
The big boy's toy!
Let me out,
Let me out,
Let me in.

12 March 1988

Suicide Mission

Suicide mission,
Dance on fire,
Dance until the end!

Suicide mission,
Suicide mission,
Dance on fire,
Dance until the end!
Suicide mission.

12 March 1988

Them and Us

Them and us.
Who are they?
Who are we?
Them and us,
Them and us,
Who are they?
Who are we?
Them and us.

12 March 1988

Children of the Stars

Children of the stars
Shine bright tonight!
Shine for me.
The sun shines for the day!
Children of the stars
Shine bright tonight!
Keep shining all through the night.
Shine for me,
Shine for us all,
Children of the stars.

4 March 1988

I.ii

1988–1991

Goodness Gracious

Good morning
Good afternoon
Good night
Goodness gracious me
Goodness gracious you
Good morning
Good afternoon
Good night

13 March 1988

Looking for Love

Once upon a time, not so long ago, there was a gladiator. A love child, who set off in search of his father. His journey took him to London, the capital of England.

He couldn't believe his eyes. The Greek gods talking and discussing the world on the British Museum at 3 a.m.

A little later he looked in the Thames and saw demons and wizards, playing with the tide. He sat and watched Big Ben, the all-telling clock of parliament. UFOs flew round the top, as shadows walked across the bridge, as if to mislead the way, but the love child was strong and walked on, with no identity in the big city.

The sun broke the dark of night. The gladiator was lost and alone; he stole cigarettes from a shop, and the fight with the law over a bright new motorcar. Found himself back in hospital, sanctuary.

The boy is waiting for the time when he will find his father, but that's another story.

8 May 1988

Peter the Potato (A Bedtime Story)

Once upon a time
A farmer put some
Potatoes in the ground.
Peter's Mum and Dad.
The rain fell
The wind blew
The sun shone
And Peter's Mum and Dad
Conceived Peter the Potato.
The flower bloomed
And the farmer pulled Peter
Out of the ground
And shipped him off to the crisp factory.
The machine chopped him
The oven cooked him
The packer packed him
And sent him off to the shops
Crunch! Somebody ate him!

4 May 1988

My Twin

He doesn't have a name
He went before we were born
He doesn't have a name
But I know him like a brother.
He sees me through life's ups and downs
He speaks to me through pop stars old and new
He sees me on the right path.
I don't talk to him
I know he's there, I feel him.
He opens doors for me
He is my twin
He doesn't have a name
He went before we were born.

25 October 1989

Our Wedding

Saturday October the fourteenth
The big day for us.
Saturday October the fourteenth
Just another day to millions.
I will give her the ring
Tell her I love her.
The best man and I
Buzz round and round
Flowers for the mums
Get me to the church on time!
Saturday October the fourteenth
Click click flash flash
The cameras go!
Phew!
Nothing to have got worried about
Saturday October the fourteenth.

25 October 1989

Blood is Blood

A door is a door!
I want to open it
Because I'm going through.
Blood is blood!
I think I've cut myself.
Wood is wood!
I want to knock on it.
Now what can I do?
Because I'm in love with you.
Curtains are curtains!
I want to open them
So the world can see
That I'm in love with you.
I believe I've got the key
To unlock life's mystery

Our Wedding

What can I do?
Because I'm in love with you
A door is a door!
Curtains are curtains!
I will open them
So the world can see
That I'm in love with you
Love with you!
Blood is blood
I cut myself
So people can see
That I'm in love with you,
Love love love
Love with you!

22 October 1989

A Game of Chess

You and I play chess every day.
We don't play to win
We play to live.
If we played to win we would
Lose all our friends.
You and I play chess every day.
We sometimes play to win
We sometimes kick the board flying
And slowly pick up the pieces.
You and I play chess every day
Some have trouble playing
Some can't play
Some are great players,
You and I play chess every day.
If you're not very good at chess
We could have a game of draughts.
We don't play to win
We play to live.

11 November 1989

Sanctuary

You are my sanctuary
You came into my life at
A time of need and loneliness
You kept my head from hitting the track
You are my sanctuary.
I came to love and care
For the love you give
You keep me from the hospital door
I don't need the sanctuary of the hospital
Now I have you to care
You are my sanctuary.
Through life's ups and downs
Parents and disappointments
You are my wife to love and to hold
You are sanctuary!

11 November 1989

The River

The river runs deep.
I look beneath the surface
To see the real you.
Some are shallow
Some are deep.
The river runs through me and you
And most things
Some deep some shallow.
Are you a drip or an ocean?
The river runs deep
Do you look beneath the surface?
Dare you?
I dare you!

13 November 1989

Love and Brotherhood

Spirit of the wind
Blow the rain into the desert
Cover the sun with clouds
Keep the light from my eyes.
Spirit of the wind
Blow the knowledge and faith
Into my life
To hide that which I found
Behind the doors!
Spirit of the wind
Blow the rain into the desert
So the world can share the winds
Love and brotherhood.
Spirit of the wind
Cover the sun with clouds.
The light sometimes hurts my eyes!

13 November 1989

A Warm Embrace

A warm embrace
A smile, a kiss
And that sparkle in your eye
Tells me this could be the time
Deep down inside
You are alive
With things beyond belief.
The seed of life is fertilised
From the one you love.
A warm embrace
A smile, a kiss
And everything's all right in the world tonight!

14 November 1989

Box No Box

Box after box
Stack after stack
Minute by minute
Hour by hour
The lines fill up.
Let's have a smoke.
Damn Geoff's here!
Fingers in the machine
Box no box
Stack no stack
The lines go down
The sun shines.
Box after box
Stack after stack
The lines fill up.

28 November 1989

Nancy

Nancy
A question a minute
Nancy
A big big nose
Nancy
Writing a book
Nancy
A question a minute
Nancy says
Smile
Smile why bloody smile
Nancy
A question a minute
Nancy
A big big nose

28 November 1989

Box No Box

Simply Simon Says

Colin says
Politics is a show!
The audience is you
Everybody knows what is what!
Some people don't realise they know.
Colin says
Good morning and good night
Have a nice dream
Help the blind to see the light
And make this world a better place.
Jesus walks in everyone
If there really was a Jesus.
Colin says
Politics is a show!
The audience is you.
Ian says
Heads will roll
Mostly politic.
Ian says
This love you found
Must never stop.
Colin says
Open your eyes
See what I see
And hear what I hear.
Ian says
Do it clean
Know what I mean?

28 November 1989

You!

You are the sunshine in my sky
The apple of my eye
You are my umbrella in the rain
Medicine when I'm in pain

You have arms to hold me
When the world turns me away
You have the key
To unlock my deepest mysteries
You are the sunshine in my sky
The apple of my eye

1 December 1989

The Forgotten Punk

In 1976 I went to art college
Back to work six months later
I needed the money.
Back to college in '77
For two years.
Punk rock was everywhere
I was a Teddy boy
But understood music
And what it could do.
Young, mixed up and confused
Anarchy and the riots
At the height of punk rock.
Finished art college
And had my first nervous breakdown.
Mixed up with politics
Fifties rockabilly
And punk rock.
It's now 1990.
I was I am
The forgotten punk!!!

5 January 1990

Mick in the Nick

I have a friend called Mick
Now he's in the nick
He had a drink
Flipped his lid
And kicked a pig.

Is his name Mick?
Anyway
He's in the nick.
Nan is concerned
But he must learn
How to drink
And think!
I have a friend called Mick
Now he's in the nick.

16 January 1990

My New Job

I've started a new job
I've been out of work since Christmas
It's now April
The start of the tax year.
The job is awful
Started Monday
Left Friday!
Can't get dole money
Worried and nervous
Must get work soon
Bloody quick!
Start work one week later
A parcel van driver
It takes me all over the UK
Liverpool
London
Newcastle
Manchester
South coast
All over the place.
I like being a van driver
Much more than
A production engineer
Drilling 4,000 holes a day!
Started Monday
Left Friday!

20 May 90

Nine Months

Six weeks to go –
The bags are packed
Boy it takes for ever
Everybody else's flies by.
Six weeks to go –
When it's your own
And you're there all the time
Boy it takes forever!
The cot is ready
The home is ready
The pusher's up her Mum's
You know the old wives' tale.
Six weeks to go –
Antenatal every two weeks
He doesn't kick so much now
He moves.
I say he
It could be she?
Six weeks to go –
The bags are packed
Boy it takes forever
When it's your own.

21 July 1990

The Nothing Girl

The girl who says nothing
When she means everything
That is the nothing girl.
We argue
Or I argue
And the nothing girl
Says nothing
And I argue more.
A tear comes to her eye

Still she says nothing
That is the nothing girl.
Maybe if she did argue
I wouldn't like what I heard
Perhaps she's too much to say
Perhaps she's nothing to say
We argue
I argue
And the nothing girl
Says nothing.
The girl who says nothing
When she means everything
That's the nothing girl.

21 July 1990

For Your Ears Only

Do you know what they sing about? It isn't always obvious, maybe I look for something that isn't really there, maybe it is, who knows?

Peace, love, Kylie and Jason sing boy–girl love songs, but Ian McCulloch and the not-so-pop pop groups get me going!

Do you know what they sing about? You and I relate to songs. I sometimes relate to a song as if it were written just for me. But that's partly what sells records, I'm sure I see things the writer never dreamt about.

In my imagination I feel as if I'm important, but what if 20,000 other fans see the same as me in McCulloch?

Do you know what they sing about? I get so frustrated to think Ian's songs are going to waste, and other great songwriters' too!

22 July 1990

For Your Ears Only

It's Good to Be Different

When you're young
It's good to be different!
I was a teenager in the seventies
Punk was different
Punk was pop!
So I had to be different again.
Rockabilly was different
I was rockabilly
Rockin' and boppin' all night!
With my flat top!
Different from Mum and Dad!
When you're young
It's important to be different.
We had our scene
Small clubs in every town
Then the boom of '81
Stray Cats, Polecats
Rockabilly turned pop!
Our scene disappeared.
When you're young
It's good to be different!!!

22 July 1990

A Lady Named Dot

Dot is my mother-in-law
She is young to be a mum-in-law
Single parent to Lucy my sister-in-law.
Dot has bad luck concerning men
Bad luck!
One beats her
One ends up in the nick
And Rob's just a kid!
A kid full of tricks
Dot is my mother-in-law
A lady named Dot!

22 July 1990

Power of Music

Grown-ups smile and dismiss music
But their children listen
Some to love songs
Get married
Find out the truth
Get divorced.
Grown-ups smile and dismiss music
But their children listen
Some to punk
Punk can fuck you up?
The kids listen
Green peace
Songs about the world
They can't change it
But the kids who listen
Are the grown-ups of tomorrow!
The power of music
Who knows?
A pop star won't be president!
But a kid will be.

28 July 1990

Through the Stars We spin

My dreams are full of magic
I can make them reality for you
For the world to see and share
In my love for you!
If people could see
Just how much I need and care
For the love you give –
My dreams are full of magic
I can make them reality for you.
We don't need psychedelic drugs
For the things we need

We only have baby
You and me!
Our dreams are full of magic
And the stars shine too
To make it all happen for me and you.
Through the stars we spin
Baby's there too
If only the world could see
My love for you and him.
Adam and Eve had the love
To make the world come true;
If only people would stop
They could share it too.
Through the stars we spin
I don't ever want to lose
The love of Jupiter, Saturn or the Magical Moon.
You may think we're on a psychedelic trip
But if you stop to think
It's only love that makes you sing.
Adam and Eve had the love
To make the world come true
So why not stop.
Look at the Moon?
You could be there too.
Through the stars we spin
I can make it reality for you.

30 July 1990

Hep Cat Bop!!!

Hep cat rock
Let's bop rock bop
With my flat top
We will rock
Hep cat bop
Till we drop
Don't stop
Hep cat rock
Let's bop rock bop
With my flat top
We will rock
To the top
We won't stop
Till we drop
Blue suede shoes
Bobby sox too
Flat top rock
Hep cat bop
All night long
Till the moonlight's gone
Hep cat rock
The morning comes
Let's bop
With my flat top
Hep cat rock
Till we drop
Don't stop
Hep cat bop

18 August 1990

Hep Cat Bop

This Green Door

Behind this green door
Is a woman in pain
This pain no man will ever know.
Behind this green door
Is a man helpless to the one he loves
A tear in his eye
As the woman in pain suffers.
Behind this green door
Is a midwife
With experience and guidance
But it's down to the woman
The woman who wishes it would end
The eternal pain that never ends.
Words cannot describe
What's behind this green door
The woman I love
I wish it would end!
Minor complications
With over three hours of pushing
The pain man will never know
Push push pant pant
And a child is born into this world.
Behind this green door
Is a woman in pain
Pain no man will ever know.

1 September 1990

Pukey Lukey

Our baby boy
Two weeks old today
He cries a little more now
But he's very good
Ten little toes
Ten little fingers
Our baby boy
Two weeks old today

Born with red hair
Quite a lot
Changing colour a bit
Blondie brown
Ten little toes
Ten little fingers
Up to 5 fl oz of milk
Our baby boy
Two weeks today
6 lb 6½ oz at birth
Now 7½ lb
That's my boy
Pukey Lukey
Two weeks old today

13 September 90

The Storm

The wind blows
The TV aerial sways all over the place
The picture's OK though.
The storm outside rages
Inside it's warm
The double-glazing keeps it out.
The wind blows
We're inland
It's not too bad.
The ship at sea
Up and down
The Coast Guard is called
The wind blows
The TV aerial sways all over the place
We're inland
It's not too bad.
Lives lost at sea
Some inland.
Inside it's warm
The double-glazing keeps it out
The wind blows
And we settle down for the night.

5 January 1991

The Cramps

Faster Pussycat
Goo Goo Muck
Human Fly
Surf with the dead
The Cramps
Give you the most
But take the least!
Can Your Pussy Do the Dog?
The way I walk
Experience the heartache
Feel the blues
Rocket to the Moon
Get Primitive
Ride the Drug Train
Put out the Garbage
The Cramps
Give you the most
But take the least!
Turn your TV knobs
As the Green Fuzz rises
Take the Mystery Plane
Lux invites you to eat some Chicken
As Ivy kills with those looks
From behind her six string
Nick hits the beat
As your bones rock to Rockin' Bones
The Cramps
Give you the most
But take the least!
Aloha from hell
Weekend on Mars
Save It
The Fever just never stops
It's just that song
You got good taste
How far can too far go?

20 January 1991

The Cramps

The Foundation of My Life

There could be no other
The love I feel
Is mostly memories
There could be no other
My grandparents
The times Grandad caught me out
We lived together
When I first went into hospital
I told Mum, Dad, all of them
They could die when they were 100 years old
Grandad wasn't well
There could be no other
He died as if to make me grow up
Nan stayed at home
But her spirit got weaker
And moved in with Mum
Nan had that look in her eyes
As if she was looking for something
Grandad never had that look
He seemed to know
I was crazy but it didn't matter
People don't understand me
There could be no other
Pop, that's Grandad, and Nan
Understood me without saying a word
My grandparents
There could be no other
Pop you're the best!
Nan I love you!
The foundation of my life

28 January 1991

I Love You!

I love you!
One million times
For every breath you take

I love you!
Two million times
For every hair on your head
I love you!
Three million times
For every drop of rain
I love you!
One million times
For every sunset
I love you!
Two million times
Each time you smile
I love you!
Three million times
Each time you look my way
I love you!
I love you!
I love you!

28 January 1991

My Parents

I don't know my blood dad
But Dad, well he's Dad.
Mum is a funny old bugger
Aren't most Mums?
Dad, like Nan
Is looking for something
Mum sees what she wants to see.
When they used to visit me in hospital
Dad would read the newspaper
Mum talked as if she knew what was what
But really didn't have a clue.
Dad, well he's Dad
Mum, the funny old bugger
I love them
I love them a lot.
They would say without a doubt
They love me
But why miss my wedding?

Our son is here now
We seem to be on top
We really hit it off!
I don't know my blood dad
But Dad, well he's Dad.
Mum is a funny old bugger
Aren't most Mums?

29 January 1991

Red

Red is for Stop!
Red is for Danger!
Green is for Go!
Amber don't know?
Fire is Red
Fire is Dangerous
When you blow your top
Hey Stop!
Red is for Stop!
Green is for Go!
If she's wearing that red dress?
Watch out
Red is Hot!
If she gives you the green light?
Hey!
Don't Stop!
Red is for stop
Red is for danger
Green is for go
Amber don't know?

29 January 1991

One of Those Nights

I lie here awake
Baby's asleep
The wife's asleep
A car goes by

Breaks the silence of midnight
Footsteps by the window
As my wife gently breathes
I lie here awake
Baby turns
Please don't wake and cry
A motorbike breaks the silence
My pen makes a shadow
Across the paper
I lie here awake
When you're tired
The light can play with your eyes
Maybe a ghost
No, just the light
A car goes by
Goodnight!
Two hours later
A car goes by
One of those nights

31 January 91

Relax

When I was in hospital, there were a couple of people who thought they were J.C. Just think what if one of them was Jesus Christ reborn? And the people of today just put him, her away.

It makes me think of the song 'Relax' by Frankie Goes to Hollywood. Here are some of the lyrics: 'Relax don't do it when you want to come'. This could mean 'Relax don't do it' – don't get excited and put away full of drugs? 'When you want to come' – when you want to show the world who you are, JC! In the song it says 'Hit me with those laser beams' – it sounds a bit like – crazy dreams!

Just think, Frankie Goes to Hollywood may not be gay, but messengers from God! After all it's one of the biggest-selling records of all time!

1 February 1991

Saturn Five '91

My baby took me on a trip last night.
We shot past the moon at 105
Spinning through the stars
Enjoying the ride.
We looped the loop round Saturn Five
Heading for the sun
With something on my mind
We hit the earth!
Ohh!!!
It was out of sight!
Good job I was wearing a condom
Safe Sex!
Don't go into orbit without one!

2 February 1991

Psycho

In 1980, my nickname was Psycho! I was one of the first at our rockabilly club to get into psychobilly music.

I used to travel to London to see the Meteors at the Hope and Anchor, Dingwalls and the 100 Club, Oxford Street.

I must admit the Meteors really hit a note with me, because they sang about mental hospitals, and I hadn't long been out of one myself!

I liked them so much I wrote two songs, 'The Mirror' and 'Saturn 5', which I took to them at the Hope and Anchor in Islington. I think they liked 'em because they talked to me a little while and said they would do them! But I never heard any more.

I can't say if the Meteors helped me with my illness or prolonged it. But it was fun being Psycho! Bal, the singer with the Stingrays (a later psycho band) will tell you how I was famous in my own little way, at our rockabilly club.

My old friends and people at the club wouldn't forget me, I was Psycho!!!

5 February 1991

Saturn Five '91

Bread and Filling

My wife and I
Are pieces of bread
And our son is the filling.
My wife's mum
Is a piece of bread
And her other daughter
The filling.
Unfortunately
My Mum-in-law's boyfriend
Isn't a piece of bread
So my Mum-in-law
Is trying to take my wife
To make her sandwich.
My wife and I
Are pieces of bread
And our son is the filling
Please keep our sandwich
Together!

6 February 1991

I.iii

1991–1996

Rain

The rain will fall
When it likes
How often it likes
Usually when you don't want it!
The rain will fall
To hide your tears
To wash your sins
To water your flowers.
The rain will fall
From heaven to earth
And turn to snow in winter.
The rain will fall
When it likes
How often it likes
To hide the sun
Or make rainbows.
The rain will fall.

8 February 1991

My Farmhouse

In 1982, there was an old house in the fields across Great Oakley. We used to look and explore inside. Then they decided to do it up! I visited the workmen one day; they must have been in a good mood because they let me look inside. I went into the cellar. Boy! Was that a posh house.

Then in 1984, I was heading for my third nervous breakdown; I walked across the fields to the house. There was a young man on a pushbike watching me; he spoke to me, and I told him to tell them the house was to be mine, I had plans for a disco in the barn. The barn was as big as the house. I often wonder what the boy must have thought of me. That night, Sunday, I went to a night club in Kettering. I hadn't put any petrol in my motor. In my foolishness I believed motor cars, etc. didn't need fuel but, just in case, I put a tin of petrol in the boot. My friend Shorty went with me. He was soon to go in the army. I danced all night, told other friends to go away rather abruptly.

Anyway we left the disco and as we got to Corby my car ran out of fuel, so I put the tin of petrol in, without a funnel! Dropped Shorty off and started heading for home. My mind was racing! Millions of thoughts and ideas a minute. So I drove to Great Oakley to try to find my farmhouse, up and down through fields and dirt tracks. An owl took off right in front of my motor. I found the house and decided to spend the night in the car. I didn't know but I had put my parking lights on; the rear light was damaged and shone a triangle on the ground. I looked at my watch: it was 11.40. Still with a million things racing through my mind, I decided I had to be home by midnight, so I left my motor and started to walk. I stopped and gave this big tree a hug. The stars were shining; I wondered which star my grandad was on. I felt one with the world – like *Star Wars*, I could feel the force! When I got home, I told Mum and Dad what I had been up to. It made sense to me, I think! Just imagine what they said and thought! So I went to bed, put my headphones on, turned up the volume, and played some records like: 'Never Stop' – the Bunnymen; 'What Difference Does It Make' – the Smiths.

Next morning, I went to get my car but, because I hadn't had a funnel to put the petrol in, it only went a couple of hundred yards. I went home; Mum took me to the doctor's and I went to the hospital! The police got my car, with my sister.

The farmhouse is finished now and somebody lives there! I often look, but only look...

10 February 1991

Party

Hey hey baby
Let's party
Party tonight
All night long
Let's party
Party now
You get the girls
I'll get the boys

Bring some booze
Food
Hey who needs food
Hey hey baby
Let's party
Party tonight
All night long
Let's party
Party now

12 February 1991

Drug Trolley

The place?
Psycho ward!
Time:
Dope-up time.
Just finished dinner
The nurse calls your name
One by one
You peer into the drug trolley
A feast of uppers downers
And screw-you-up drugs.
Kemadrin are gold dust!
They are for side effects
If it's not on your card
You don't get 'em
You shake, dribble and feel
so insecure it's unbelievable.
Depending what drugs you're on
The lack of Kemadrin
Can really screw you up.
Time:
Dope-up time
The place?
Psycho ward!
Take your turn at the drug trolley.

12 February 1991

Motorway Madness

I used to be a parcel van driver
Up and down the motorways I went
In my Mercedes 307 D
Foot down!
It wasn't mine
1.30 a.m. to Glasgow
M6 all the way
Birmingham asleep
Kent
M11 M25 Dartford Tunnel
Plymouth
M4 M5 foot down
Police patrol
Hey ease up
Motorway Madness
I used to be a parcel van driver
Up and down and back again
In my Mercedes 307 D

17 February 1991

You Blow My Mind

Hey baby you blow my mind
Put me into gear
And we'll reach the stars
We'll blast past the moon and Saturn Five
To the four corners and beyond
I'll cover you in flowers
Make honey for the bees
Send the birds to the trees
Ride the hurricane!
Swim the depths of the oceans
Populate Venus and Mars
Change gear from fourth to first – first to third
And watch the rev counter spin
Blast past the moon and Saturn Five

To the four corners and beyond
Populate Venus and Mars
Baby you blow my mind

21 February 1991

Bad Management

In June and July of 1990, I talked with Jenny Colman, manager of the parcel van department at the transport and warehousing firm I worked for, about having a week off when my baby was born and my wife came out of hospital. She said just let her know when and it would be OK. Towards the end of August, Jenny and I talked about my week off quite often because it was getting close. On Wednesday 29 August, my wife went into labour. I phoned Jenny that morning to tell her I wouldn't be in work and why. My son was born the next day and I went back to work on Friday 31st of August. I then said to Jenny I would need the following week off as we had discussed. She then said I had to ask Mr Hunt, managing director of the firm, about my week off which Jenny, my manager, had already said I could take off. So I went to see Mr Hunt that afternoon, Friday 31 August. His secretary told me he was out; I waited two-and-a-quarter hours for him. In this time I had been talking to my foreman about my week off. I could not wait any longer for Mr Hunt as I wanted to see my wife and son in hospital. As my manager and foreman knew about my week off, and Jenny had already told me it would be OK, I went home and had the week off to take care of my wife. Jenny phoned me at home 6 a.m. Monday morning, as if she didn't know anything about my situation, to see if I was coming to work. I went back to work Monday 10 September and was called in to see Mr Hunt, where I was given one week's notice for not informing management about my baby and my week off, which was all I'd talked about for weeks with my manager Jenny Colman.

22 February 1991

Heartache

Heartache
Heartache
Pain
Heartache
Heartache
Pain

Do you know?
Heartache
Leave it all behind
Heartache
Paracetamol
Aspirin
Heartache
Take the lot!
Choke
Throw up
Heartache
Start again
Paracetamol
Aspirin
It never works
Feel like shit!
Hallucinating
Heartache
Heartache
Pain
Do you know?
Heartache
Heartache
Pain
Heartache

January 1992

Jesus in My Head

Jesus give me strength
Jesus give me hope
To get through this my longest day.
Each day gets longer
Jesus give me strength
Till the pain goes away.
My Jesus is my music!
My music is my friend
I have a song for all my different moods.
Jesus give me strength
Jesus give me hope

If the Church had the money
Which I have spent on music
The Church would be a lot wealthier
But this is the nineties
And the Church doesn't come into it.
Jesus give me strength
Jesus give me hope
On this my longest day.
I see a light
Is it Jesus?
No!
It's a record shop
Jesus in my head.

February 1992

Lonely

Have you ever been lonely?
Do you know what it is like?
To be in a crowd
But still alone.
You say hello to a stranger
Or someone you vaguely know
Hoping and praying for a reply.
Have you ever been lonely?
Fed up with your TV
So you hit the streets
For a walk
People laughing and joking
With their friends
But still you're lonely.
People in and out of pubs and clubs
You look to the night sky
Hoping and praying
For that special friend
The friend who will share your dreams
Maybe that friend feels like you tonight?
Is he she looking at the same star?
Have you ever been lonely?
Do you know what it's like?

You yearn to meet that friend
The friend to share your dreams.

Easter 1992

HMV

She lives not far from here
But where I don't know.
I stand here and dream
Dream of the past
Dream of the future
The girls I've loved and lost
Spring is just around the corner
Maybe this year
Please this year!
A kindred spirit
For me to love
To share my world
My world is big
My world is small
Let me!
Let me walk through your garden
Smell your perfume
Let me dive into your ocean
And as I come up for air
I will give you the key
The key to unlock my innermost mysteries
Where does she live?
I really don't know
Maybe I don't want to know
Maybe I'm scared
You see
I'm running out of keys
And deep mystery

31 January 1993

The Chosen One

I'm the one!
The one on the torpedo
I'll ride this torpedo till the very end!
I'm the chosen one
Chosen before birth!
Chosen at conception
This torpedo
This torpedo is guided
Guided through life
Love and lost
Love and guided
Door to door
Pulled back from beyond!
And pushed again
Many green doors
I'm the one!
The one on the torpedo
Guided by beacons
Beacons strong beacons weak
Chosen!
Chosen before birth
Chosen at conception

February 1993

Ozone

Ozone ozone
O-no not my ozone
Don't smoke near my ozone
Ozone ozone
Not my ozone
The child's ozone
Will be gone
When the ozone blown

The kids must live
When the ozone gone
Ozone ozone
O-no not my ozone
Don't smoke near the kid's ozone
Ozone ozone
Not my ozone

1993

Roller Coaster

I'm on this roller coaster
I cannot get off
No one can hear you scream!
The roller coaster is empty
I see a light
The coaster speeds up
Help!
Help!
It's lonely
No one to hear you scream!
Ghost from the past
Ghost to the future
I can't get off
The ride is long
The end is near
And in your arms
I feel no fear

6 February 1993

One Day Soon

One day
One day soon
I will fly to you
Across the seven seas
And the Atlantic too
One day soon

I will be with you
I will touch you
I will give you hope
I will make you new
Set you free
Break the chains of
                    government's corruption
                    and propaganda
One day
One day soon
I will be with you

6 February 1993

In My Head to My Mind

In my head to my mind
The things you said
My mind is big
My mind is small
Red your head
My head too
The things you said
Went completely to the dead
And the unfed
In my head
The things you said

8 February 1993

The Jigsaw

Down and out
Rich and famous
Rich and famous
Down and out
Pilot of Concorde
Pushing my pushbike

In My Head to My Mind

All pieces
Pieces in the puzzle
The jigsaw
Jigsaw of life

4 March 1993

English Rabbits

Run rabbit run
I'll have you tomorrow
On my plate
Run rabbit run
I'll string you up
When the moonlight's gone
The sun is high
Run rabbit run
For your life
We are the hunters
Run rabbit run
Run rabbit run
Run run run
With your blue 'n' red jackets on

1993

Robert

There was a man from Wackenhut
Who worked at Kettering General
He sorted out some of the people
And some of them went mental

14 April 1993

Peacock

If I were a peacock
And you were a bumblebee

Your kiss would be heavenly to me.
If I were a peacock
And you were a wasp
Your kiss would mean death for me.
If I were a peacock
And you were a bee
Your love would be twins for me.
If I were a peacock
And you were a bee
I would lift my feathers
For all to see.

10 May 1993

Thunderbird Heaven

They come from near
They come from far
Oxford, Tennessee, the USA
I wish they would stay
Top of the Pops
What a flop!
Thunderbird Heaven
Oxford, Tennessee, the USA
Thursday night we pray
They come from near
They come from far
Oh boy what a star!
Steve and Lee
Spin the CDs
On the river bank
So near so far
Rave on to be a star!
Elvis sings
Don't be cruel
Back to school
They come from near
They come from far
Wellingborough
Full of stars!
Bop jive

Twist and shout
Let it out
Up down around and around
Slow fast
Don't be last

13 May 1993

Cathy's Clown

'Cathy's Clown'
Number one
The week I was born!
Cathy O Cathy
Took my innocence
She didn't know
Took my virginity
Luton Airport
Cathy's Clown

14 May 1993

Hey Girl

Hey girl
You don't need me!
Hey woman
You don't need me!
Hey girl
What's in the bedside drawer?
Hey girl
Let me show you how!
Hey woman
I won't let you down!
Hey woman
I'm the best around!
Hey girl
Hey woman
Don't open that drawer
The boys are back in town!

Hey girl
You don't need me!
Hey woman
You don't need me!
Hey girl
What's that in the bedside drawer?

23 May 1993

Reflections

Monday night
Monday night
And we head for Reflections!
Different walks of life
Pound in!
Pound a drink!
Monday night
Monday night
Students' night!
Reflections from the past
Reflections to the future
From the past
And don't be last!
This Monday night
I danced
Danced with a young girl
Is it me?
But she looked so young!
I had to run
Monday night
Monday night
Oh to be young!
Reflections of today
I wish they'd go away
She's so young!
I need to run

24 May 1993

Maria

She lies beside me!
Soft and gentle
Twitches
Twitches at the movie
She lies beside me!
Soft and gentle
I massage her hand
Pins and needles you see
Still no kiss
The kiss I would die for
She lies beside me!
Soft and gentle
When you're young love comes and goes
As you mature love gets harder
You forget the game
She lies beside me!
Soft and gentle
The kiss I would die for
Marie, Marie
The kiss I long for!!!

24 May 1993

One Sunny Afternoon

Walking home from school
One sunny afternoon
Who's car is that?
Outside my house
Walking home from school
Up the garden path
This sunny afternoon
It's him!
It's gotta be him
My Dad
Natalie smiles
Her smile turns to excitement!!!

Walking home from school
One sunny afternoon

25 May 1993

Trish

How's tricks Trish
How's the kids Trish
How's tricks Trish
How's the kids Trish
Your tricks are the pits
Pits pits tricks pits
How's tricks Trish
How now Miss Brown
See you around
But not in town
Tricks Trish and the kids

25 May 1993

Growing Pain

Schizophrenic voices
Schizophrenic thoughts
Psychedelic voices
Psychedelic thoughts
Growing pains
Miscarriage
Why?
Pain pain pain!!
Growing pains
Schizophrenic drugs
Psychedelic drugs
Growing pains
Take a trip here
Take a trip there
Growing pains
The birth of your son!
The birth of your daughter!

Why?
Why the pain?
The one you love
Hurts you
Kicks you, lifts you
Schizophrenic voices
Schizophrenic thoughts
Psychedelic voices
Psychedelic thoughts
Pain pain!
Growing pains
Why?
Pain

26 May 1993

Christine

Run run run!!!
Gas up and run
Christine my motorcar
Christine my gal
She gives me erections
Run run run!!!
Gas up and run
Here comes the law
But what for?
Run gal run
When Christine is ill
I worry
Worry it could be the end
My brother Adam
Adam makes her new
Run run run!!!
Gas up and run
We're off again!
Liverpool
London
Guided by love
Love and Jupiter
Saturn Five not tonight!

Run run run!!!
Gas up and run
Christine my motorcar
Christine my gal
Christine my lover
Christine my love
Soon to part
She'll break my heart!

26 May 1993

Another Lonely Night

As I lie in my bed
In my bedsit
I struggle for inspiration
With all my creature comforts around me
Material goodies
Material goodies I have worked for!
Shadows dance
Dance from object to object.
Top and Hendrix, my pet rats,
Squeak and make love.
Tomorrow soon to come
Tomorrow another day
Another lonely night.
One night
One night soon!
I will have a love of my own
She will squeak
I will squeak
and the shadows
Will be the shadows of love.
As I lie in my bed
In my bedsit
I struggle for inspiration
And a love all of my own.

30 May 1993

Love Hate

Love hate
Love hate
Tell me the difference?
People I should hate
Really hate
I don't
If I don't hate anyone
Can I love anyone?
Love hate
Love hate
The fool that stole my family
One I should hate!
I don't
I believe
I believe for every negative
There is a positive
Circles
Circles in and out
And back again
Love hate
Love hate
As sure as my boy was taken
Time will bring him back
Circles
Life's little circles
Love hate
Love hate
Can I love anyone?
I don't feel hate
Believe me I'm no saint

13 June 1993

Oh Little Girl

Little girl
Oh little girl

I love you so!
Please don't go!
He may have money
I know we can't live on dreams alone
Little girl
Oh little girl
I know you love me so
Are my dreams so impossible?
I will dream
Dream till they come true.
Little girl
Oh little girl
I love you so!
Why'd ya make me go?
Nobody knows our story
Nobody ever will!
That's our bitter pill.
I must go
I'll always love you so!!!

17 July 1993

I Wrote a Few Poems

I wrote a few poems!
I wrote to the *NME* and McCulloch
Circulating my ideas
Ideas of a better life
Life for everyone and myself.
I wrote a few poems
Married and divorced
But kept on going
Until the big one!
All eyes looking at me
The media machine made me number one
Number one for a couple of months
Spring 1993!
Being number one is a feeling
What to do with this feeling?
Empty headed I walked the streets
Up and down

And back again
The streets of Kettering.
I had a good job!
A couple of friends
It's now winter '93
No job!
Not so many friends
The feelings have gone!
I wrote a few poems
But what for
What for?

24 October 1993

A Cup of Tea

Polly put the kettle on!
We will all drink tea.
In goes the tea bag
Hot water!
Boiling hot water.
Polly put the kettle on!
We will all drink tea.
In goes the sugar
Stardust from the cane.
Polly put the kettle on;
In goes the milk
Squeeze the bag.
Polly put the kettle on!
We will all drink tea.
Oh I wanted coffee.

25 October 1993

It's Up to You

I've been mixed up
I've been down
I've been high
I've been places you wouldn't like to know

But after all is said and done
It's up to you!
You're on your own
I've been down so long
It's up to me
I've been mixed up
I've been high
It's great being high
But as sure as you went up
You're going to come down
It's up to you!
It's up to you to find yourself
Find yourself in the ups and down
It's up to you!
You're on your own
Up down and all around

26 October 1993

Can You Cope?

Can you cope?
People laughing
People crying
Can you cope?
Are you in control?
In control of your body and soul?
Do you notice?
People laughing
People crying
Do you manipulate people?
Do they manipulate you?
Can you cope?
People laughing
People crying
Can you cope?

26 October 1993

Time is the Answer

You can't go on
You must go on
You have to go on!
Time is the biggest healer
You don't have time
The pain is too great
You can't go on
You must go on
You have to go on!
Spit in their face
Kick in the eye
Fight for your life
Make time!
For time is the answer
You must go on
You have to go on!

20 May 1996

Just a Memory

She's gone
She's been gone years
I don't think of her so often
She's gone
It's almost as if she was never there
The girl I loved
The girl I married
She's gone
The hurt and the pain has gone
She's gone
The woman
The woman who gave me a son
I think of him
But he's gone too
Out of my life
What do I do?

I have one thing
One thing nobody can take
That's the memory
It's just a memory
She's gone
And the memory is slowly going too
The girl I loved
Who?

21 May 1996

Ashtray

Ashtray
Ashtray
You stink
Ashtray
I fill you up
I empty you
I wash you
Ashtray
Ashtray
You stink
Ashtray
My smelly socks
Sorry that's another poem
Ashtray
Ashtray
You stink
Ashtray

21 May 1996

I.iv

1996–1998

Pillow

Pillow you're soft
Pillow you're there
You hold my head
You rest my neck
You're on my bed
She comes and she goes
But pillow you're there
On my bed
To rest my neck
I sometimes wonder who's best
Sorry pillow!
No contest
Pillow you're soft
Just hold my head
And rest my neck
Pillow!

21 May 1996

I Remember

It happened yesterday
Yesterday along time ago!
I was the man
The man everybody talked about
They say I imagined the lot
I know different
Some were scared
Some were embraced
Some uplifted
Times change

I remember
I'll never forget
The man from yesterday
Yes it was me!
It happened yesterday
Yesterday along time ago!

22 May 1996

A Little Mystery

We wander life's highway
Some without a thought
Without any trouble or mystery.
We wander life's highway
Some question everything
Full of troubled thoughts and mystery
Some are deep
Some are shallow
Why do we look for answers?
For every answer poses another question.
We wander life's highway
We are born
And we die
Who's better off?
Those deep in thought
Those without trouble or mystery.
It's romantic to be deep and in mystery
As you mature and grow
Personally I think!
Hey what the heck.
We wander life's highway
Who knows?
I certainly don't.
As you mature and get older
I've realised
Hey it doesn't matter
And I wander life's highway
Without a troubled thought
But still
A little mystery.

26 May 1996

PSMS

I never loved you
I lived with you
I made love with you
But I never loved you
You helped me
Helped me get over my wife
Sort out my life
Sorry!
I never loved you
I never could.
Your family, Mum, Sister-in-law
Sick and twisted;
Your kids
Drove me half nuts.
I never loved you
I lived with you
I made love with you.
But I never loved you

27 May 1996

Labyrinth

The mind is a labyrinth
With hidden depths
Doors open
Doors close
The mind is a labyrinth
Some are at peace
Some a circus
The circus races round
You cannot sleep
The mind is a labyrinth
Which you must control
Find the peace
And you will sleep
The mind is a labyrinth
With hidden depths

Doors open
Doors close
The mind is a labyrinth

29 May 1996

It's You!

Skip in the meadow
Run naked through the wind
Break the chains
Free your spirit
For it's you
And you alone!
Unlock the doors
Run naked through the wind
Climb the highest mountain
Swim the deepest river
Dance in the rain
For it's you
And you alone!

4 June 1996

Thunder!

Can you hear it calling?
The thunder in the sky
Far far away
Calling
Calling your name
Lightning fills the sky
The thunder bangs and crunches
Louder and louder
Over your head
What do you want?
It screams your name
Louder and louder
What do you want?
The lights go out

A power cut
Are you scared?
Are you embraced?
Do you hear it calling
Calling your name?
It's pouring with rain
It's always the same

5 June 1996

Empty

It's gone!
There's nothing left
My head is empty
My life is empty
I used to dream
The dream has gone
It's gone!
There's nothing left
I dreamt of a better life
I dreamt I was to save the planet
I laugh at myself
How?
Silly fool
It's gone!
There's nothing any more
I can't even save myself
My head is empty
My life is empty
Don't look to me
I can't help you
It's gone!
Well gone
Looking back
I never had any answers
The only one I was fooling was me
My head is empty
My life is empty
I used to dream
The dream has gone

I'm boring
I'm bored!

28 October 1996

You Don't Know

You don't know
You don't know
How much I need
Your soft skin
Your warm embrace
I go crazy
End up ill
With loads of pills
You don't know
You don't know
You're everything
I'm nothing
Nothing but a nervous wreck
I need you in my bed
I'm not talking about sex
You don't know
You don't know
How much I need
Your soft skin
Your warm embrace
I go crazy
End up ill
With loads of pills
You don't know

28 October 1996

I Really Do!

You are like the wind
A breath of fresh air
On a summer spring morning
Your eyes sparkle
Like the stars in the sky
You turn me on
Like a child turns the light switch
Your love is endless
Love you
I love you
Like the wind
That blows across the sea
The birds and bees
Were made for you and me
Let's plant a tree
To reach the stars
I'm in heaven
In your arms
You are like the wind
A breath of fresh air
Love you
I love you
On this winter's morning
Our love is just dawning
Love you
Love you
I really do!
Love you

12 November 1996

The Skitzo Man

The skitzo man comes
The skitzo man goes
Where he comes from
Where he goes to

Nobody knows for sure
He talks to himself
He's very kind and gentle
He means you no harm
The skitzo man comes
The skitzo man goes
Try to imagine
Wonder how it must be
A circus in your head
Ten twenty thoughts all at once
Living day after day with medication
Feeling up down and sideways
The skitzo man comes
The skitzo man goes
Where he comes from
Where he goes to
Nobody knows for sure
Could this be you?
The skitzo man

15 November 1996

The Eyes

Are you alone?
I am alone
But the eyes
The eyes watch you!
Everything you do
Everywhere you go
Are you alone?
I am alone
But the eyes
The eyes!
You draw your curtains
I am alone
But the ears
The ears listen!
I must get away
Away!
Away from the eyes

Away from the ears
But where?
Are you alone?
I am alone
But the eyes
The ears
You cannot escape
The eyes
The eyes follow you
The ears listen to your every move
Are you alone?
I am alone
But the eyes
The eyes!

16 November 1996

They're Here

The aliens are here
They have always been here
They live among us
Work among us
Breed among us
They watch
They wait
They wait for him
The man
The man among men
The aliens are here
I know
I have seen them
They have shown themselves to me
The aliens are here
They watch
They wait
Some have power in society
Most are like you and me
Walking down the street
Cooking the Sunday dinner
The aliens are here

No need for alarm
They'll do you no harm
Like you and me
They look for answers
They look
They wait
They're here

20 November 1996

Love Fact or Fiction

Does love exist?
I believe it must
But few find it
It can make you bitter
Cynical
Everybody needs love
Everybody looks for love
The cynical
Believe it doesn't exist
The older bitter person
Can believe
It's a teenage dream
Does love exist?
Yes it does
Yes yes!!
But few find it
If love doesn't exist
How come there's so many broken hearts
Does love exist?
I believe it does
For my heart is in pieces
Does love exist?
Oh yes
It exists!

27 November 1996

Tight Blue Jeans

There is a lady
A lady in my life
I want her
I need her
She's not what she seems!
I see her most days
We chat
Drink tea
She's everything to me!
There is a lady
A lady in my life
She turns me on
She's a friend
That's all it can be
I want her
I need her
She's not what she seems!
We have no secrets
We say what we feel
We love music
I want her
I need her
She's not what she seems!
The lady in the tight blue jeans

13 December 1996

In Love with a Lesbian

She never led me on
I knew from the start
I'm the fool
The fool in love
In love with a lesbian
I look in her eyes
I see warmth
Love

Affection
For me, I don't think so
I misread all the signs
Jumped in feet first
The pool was too deep
No one to bail me out
She never led me on
I knew from the start
Yes I'm the one
The one in love
In love with a lesbian
She's kind
Thoughtful
Hurting
Hurting for love
But not my love
I'm the fool
The fool who thought
It could be me
She never led me on
I'm the fool
The fool
In love with a lesbian
She never stole my heart
I just threw it away

22 December 1996

Star

Star in the night sky
You shine so very bright
What secrets do you hide?
Star in the night sky
So very far away
Are you all alone?
Up there shining bright
Among thousands of stars.
Star in the night sky
I sit here
Alone

People come and go
But I'm still alone.
I wonder star
How you must feel
Star in the night sky
Up there all alone
You shine so very bright
What secrets do you hide?
Star in the night sky.

14 January 1997

Torment

I sit here alone
Thinking of the days
The days when love was easy
A different girl every week
I sit here alone
Longing, hurting for love
I imagine time after time
How it would be
Slowly undressing a woman
Discovering a new body
The soft touch of her skin
The sweet smell of her perfume
I sit here alone
Tormenting myself
Only I can change my situation
I know she's out there
I sit here alone
Hurting, longing
Thinking of the days
The days long gone
I sit here alone
In torment!!!

18 January 1997

Sex

If you haven't got it
You want it
When you get it
You think
Is that it?
TV, pop songs, Hollywood
Create the myth
It's drummed into you
It's what it's all about
If you haven't got it
You want it
You need it
When you get it
You think
Is that it?
That's it
You soon forget
You want it again
Sex
Sex is a con
Love
Love can be different
Few find love
Love hurts
Sex
Sex is fun
Sex is frustrating
You want it
You need it
Sex is a con
If you haven't got it
You want it
Sex!

24 March 1997

Sex

Dreams, Ideas

Dreams, ideas
Where did they go?
A walk up town
A walk in the woods
Nothing left
Nothing to discover
Married, divorced
Your baby's first breath
The innocence of life
I don't want my childhood back
I just wish something would happen
Dreams, ideas
Most withered and faded
No mystery
Going through the motions
Day-in, day-out
Dear God, Jesus, anyone
Give me a purpose
Warmth, love
Something that's me
Dreams, ideas
Where did they go?
Need motivation
Motivation from within
Something that's me
Dreams, ideas!

26 March 1997

I'm Not Jesus

I'm not Jesus
I fool no one
Is there a God up above?
Who knows?
What if

What if Jesus did appear?
Who would listen
What could he say
What could he do
I'm not Jesus
The TV
The radio
Told me I was
I can't heal a cripple!
I've never read the Bible
You have your story
I have my story
One day we will all be dead
Just give me my medication
And I'll be on my way
I'm not Jesus

18 July 1997

Elaine

She is at the Bungalow
In her bright and colourful clothes
Nothing is too much
A ray of sunshine on a winter's day
She makes a cup of tea
With a smile, never a frown
She is at the Bungalow
If you're down
She'll pick you up
She plays the guitar
With a smile and a song
Nothing is too much
In her bright and colourful clothes
Elaine
Elaine
At the Bungalow!

22 July 1997

I'm Not Looking!

I don't want a woman
I'm not looking!
I listen to songs
I listen to songs about women
Songs about love
The glory
The downfall
I don't want a woman
Is there something wrong with me?
I don't think so
I'm set in my ways
Love
Love is a memory
Love hurts
Love is great
What's wrong with me?
Nothing
Nothing at all
Tomorrow's another day
Maybe
Maybe not
I don't want a woman
I'm not looking!

2 August 1997

I'm Not Schizophrenic!?

I'm not schizophrenic
The TV
The radio
I was famous
Famous with no name!
It's boring now
My fame has passed
It tortures me
The thought that it really happened

I'm not schizophrenic
Life becomes so boring and meaningless
After the high
The high of it all happening
It's happened a few times
Never really left me
But now it's gone
It's true
Nothing lasts for ever!
I'm not schizophrenic
I wish I were
The TV
The radio
I was famous
I sit here
With my memories
Memories that torture
I'm not schizophrenic
I never was
'Coz
Well
Just because!

28 September 1997

A Dark Cloud

A dark cloud crossed the UK today
A lump in my throat
A shiver down my back
The one we admire
Taken from us
I pray for her
I pray for her two boys
Taken so young
She touched the hearts of so many.
A dark cloud came over the UK today
Outside my front door
It's just like any other day
The BBC broadcast nothing else
The one we admire

Taken from us
I pray for her
She will always be
Our queen of hearts
A dark cloud
A shiver down my back
Came over us today.

31 August 1997

Let's Go Faster!!!

Here we go!
One hundred
Two hundred
Faster, faster
No breaks
Three hundred
Four hundred
Here we go!
No sleep tonight
Wild as the wind
Thunder, lightning
Faster, faster
Over the top
And down below
One hundred
Two hundred
Faster 'n' faster
We've only just begun
Three hundred
Four hundred
Faster 'n' faster
Breaks
Who needs breaks?
Where are we going?
Who knows?
Faster
Let's go faster
Five hundred
Six hundred

They'll never catch us
Faster, faster
Let's go faster!!!

3 September 1997

The Shave

Are you looking at me?
I'm looking at you
What do you see?
I see a face
What do you see?
I see a tired man
Are you looking at me?
I'm looking at you
I see a boy
A child in my eyes
What do you see?
I see whiskers
Whiskers that need a shave
That's what I see
Look up you fool
I don't want to be cut
Are you looking at me?
I'm looking at you
What do you see?
I see a tired face
Goodnight!
Hey!
What about the teeth?
What about the teeth?

3 September 1997

The Shave

Dear Mother

Oh Mother
What can we do?
To lighten the load
You complain day after day
You have your children's children
Running round and round
Oh Mother
What can we do?
If you never had your grandkids
You would complain
You complain and feel ill anyway
Oh Mother
What can we do?
I can't lighten the load
I can't make you well
We all love you
I hope it's not too late
Before you get what you want
What is it you want?
Because you're not happy
Oh Mother
What can I do?
You complain about this
You complain about that
How can we make you happy?
Happy and content
If it's not this
It's that
Oh Mother
Dear Mother!!!

4 September 1997

It Will Never Be!

It will never be
The affection I feel

I don't kid myself
Dream
I do dream
She likes me I think
She has affection for me
It will never be
Her work stops everything
I've known her many years
Why do I fall for those I can't have?
It will never be
I see her most days
We chat
Discuss this and that
Her work stops everything
Dream
I do dream
It will never be

9 September 1997

Nina

Nina O Nina
You're on the move
Up and away
I wish you would stay
You will surely be missed
But your decision is made
And you cannot stay
Nina O Nina
You leave many friends and memories
But with your sunshine personality
Many new friends will come your way
Nina O Nina
I wish you would stay
But you're up and away

2 October 1997

The Tide

The tide is high
The tide is up
You're up against it
You're swimming for your life
The tide is strong
The tide is a feeling
A feeling you must fight
The tide is high
The tide is up
The tide comes and goes
Sometimes stronger than other times
The tide is a feeling
A feeling of suicide
Deep down inside
Heartache, but not always
Life, life is a bitch
The tide comes in
The tide goes out
You're up against it
You're swimming for your life
The tide is high
The tide is up

2 October 1997

Stop and Think!

Do you ever stop?
Stop and think
Think about petrol etc
One day it will be gone
Maybe not tomorrow
But one day!
Hundreds and thousands
Of motor vehicles
Up and down the highway
All with their precious bit of fuel

Do you ever stop?
Stop and wonder
Wonder in disbelief
How long it took to make
Gone in seconds
Never to be seen again
Next time you're filling up
Stop and think!
One day it will be gone
Do you ever give it a thought?
Do you ever stop?
Stop and think

15 October 1997

No One

I don't have love
I need love
I would die for love
Crawl on my hands and knees
My life is empty
I am lost
Lost and all alone
I long for that touch
Warmth that only a woman can give
I don't have love
I need love
I would die for love
I wander life's highway
Lost and alone
The feeling goes deep inside
The flame flickers
It's nearly dead
What can I do?
The perfume
The smell of a woman
Is just a memory
I don't have love
I need love
I would die for love

Love
What is love?
The flame is dead
I keep hanging on
There just is no one
No one to love
No one

30 November 1997

Love Above

Woman full of love
You pray to God above
Leave me in the cold
Woman full of warmth
Never to come my way
Maybe I should pray
We danced the night away
Now I'm on my own
Waiting for the phone
Woman full of love
For Jesus up above
I cannot wait for tomorrow
To see those smiling eyes
When I see you
I must go!
Because I love you so
It hurts to know
It's all for Jesus above
You wait for heaven on earth!
A belief I cannot grasp
So I don't ask
Woman full of love
Not to come my way
Maybe I should pray
Today!

8 December 1997

Meaning of Life!?

At some time in your life
You will look for answers
The meaning of life.
Every answer found
Creates another question.
One day
You will find the key
The key
To set your mind at ease
Set your spirit free.
At some time in your life
You question
The meaning of life.
Few never find the key
Some don't look
But when you open that door
It's like a ton weight
Lifted from your shoulders.
The secret is
There is no secret
And the meaning of life
Is a bright shining light
Inside your mind.
Meaning of life
Goodnight
Sleep tight
Tonight.

14 December 1997

Spirit of Jesus

I'm not Jesus
But the spirit
The spirit of Jesus
Is in me.
It's in you too,
You must look deep inside.

If you're a bad person
You have to look a bit deeper
Unfortunately
Satan
Satan is in there too.
It's the old story
Good against evil
Like a children's cartoon.
Don't be afraid but
It's no cartoon.
One day soon
Jesus will come
The spirit of Jesus
And Satan cast to hell
It will be heaven on earth.
The spirit of Jesus
Is in me
He's in you too
Spirit of Jesus.

14 December 1997

Two by Two

Two by two
We all go together
Don't panic
She is out there
He is out there
Two by two
We all go together
Forget the past
Now is the time
Don't panic
It's not too late
It's gonna last
Two by two
We board the boat
It will float
It's no joke

17 December 1997

My Heart Did Know!

Many moons ago
My heart did know
When I was six
When I was seven
I looked up at heaven
Many moons ago
My heart did know

17 December 1997

Big Ben

Two thousand and ten
I saw Big Ben
Tick tock
Tick tock
Around the clock
Two thousand and ten
I saw Big Ben
It wasn't the end

4 January 1998

I.v

1998–1999

Buzzy Bee!

Buzzy Bee oh! Buzzy Bee
Slow down Bumble Bee
Relax you silly Buzzy Bee
Bumble Bee says
Leave me alone!
I know my pace
Bumble Bee oh! Bumble Bee
Slow down Buzzy Bee
Bumble Bee

15 January 1998

Sweet Little Sixteen

Pregnant at twelve
Smoking at thirteen
Drunk at fourteen
Dead at fifteen
What ever happened to
Sweet little sixteen?

14 January 1998

Kiss and Run

Kiss and Run!
What a lot of fun
Oh those girls
Scream and shout!

Kiss and Run!
What fun
The kiss they like best
Is the one that makes 'em wet!

31 January 1998

Rip Off!

I don't believe in God!
God wouldn't have ripped me off
Only people do that
They fill you full of dreams
Then never deliver.
I don't believe in God!
God wouldn't have ripped me off.

1 February 1998

Kate

There is a young woman
Who fills my prescriptions
She writes me little notes
If this young woman
Was in my life
I probably wouldn't need
Need so many prescriptions
Because love is all you need
You could be my medication!
The love I have to give
The love is endless
It could be for this woman
Who writes me little notes
How I'd love those notes
To be notes of love
There is a young woman
Who fills my prescriptions
A woman

A woman called
Kate

February 1998

Size Tens

Standing in my size tens!
I looked at Big Ben
With clouds all around
The sun does shine
Standing in my size tens!
I look down and around
People in a hurry
People with nothing to do
Everyone sings the blues
Standing in my size tens!
The world is really quite small
I look up, I look down
Around and around
Everybody knows the truth
Apart from me and you
Standing in my size tens!
I looked at Big Ben
The End!

11 February 1998

Empty World!

I have nothing!
Nothing to interest me
My world is empty
I gave the world my soul
They laughed
I have nothing
My poems are jokes
My soul is worthless
I am empty
Inside out
Inside out

In an inside out
Empty world

18 February 1998

Nicky

Last-minute decision
Trip to cashpoint
Money in pocket
Off we go!!!
Rock 'n' roll bop jive
Thunderbird
Oh! What a night
Young woman
Father and uncle in tow
Oh boy!
What a gal
Here goes
Would you like to dance?
I can't dance
That's OK I can't dance
Last-minute decision
Trip to cashpoint
Money in pocket
Off we go!
Bop Jive
Twist and Shout!
A kiss goodnight
I wait for the phone
I'm like a dog
Without his bone
I wonder if she's alone?

21 March 1998

Still Here!

I sit here with my dreams
Looking out the window
With dreams that are fading

Just fading away!
I'm not a religious person
But like the Jehovah's Witness
I dreamt of heaven
Heaven on earth.
I sit here with my dreams
Dreams of tomorrow
No more fighting
My dreams are pie in the sky.
I look out of my window
My dreams are misplaced
My dreams are fading
Just fading away!
But I'm still here
Still here…

24 April 1998

Only You!

Some think they have you sussed
Know your thoughts
Have worked out your moods.
Some think they're clever
When really they know nothing!
Some take you for granted
Day in day out
They see what they want to see
Can they see the pain?
The love?
The universe spins round inside your heart and soul
You laugh, you joke!
To hide the pain
The love
The love of life.
You could talk
Talk for days, weeks
Still they wouldn't know
So you laugh, you joke!
Some think they have you sussed
Know your thoughts

Your moods!
When only you
Only you know
Your pain!
Your love!
Your life!

10 August 1998

The Woods

Have you seen the Teddies?
The Teddies in the woods
The Teddy bears' picnic.
I've seen the squirrels
I've seen the starling
I've seen the lovers
Hand in hand
Walking through the woods
But Teddies
I've never seen
The Teddies.
I've felt the breeze
Watched the leaves fall
Seen the flowers bloom
The gentle flowing spring
But Teddies
I've never seen
The Teddies
The Teddy Bears' picnic!

18 August 1998

Nothing for You

I'm a sad person
A sad miserable old bugger.
Inside I'm happy
But when I think of my children
I'm sad to say the least.
My daughter wrote to me

We spent some time together
I had not a lot to say
Nothing to give her
No words of wisdom.
It makes me frustrated
Frustrated and sad
When I think of my son
The day he may look for me.
I'm a sad miserable old bugger
I have nothing
I wish I had
I have nothing
Nothing for you...

30 August 1998

Living on the Edge

I have loads of CDs
Approximately four-hundred pop/indie
Four-hundred rockin'
Rockabilly, rock 'n' roll, psychobilly.
My rockin' music keeps me sane
It sings about nothing
You can dance and have a laugh.
When I play my pop/indie music
I go somewhere I can't explain
It can be scary
It's taken me over the edge many times
Yes O/D myself.
All my life or as long as I can remember
I have had this illness they call schizophrenia.
I laugh I joke
When really I'm living on the edge.
Rock 'n' roll rockabilly pulls me back
It sings about nothing
Music is my life
Living on the edge!

22 September 1998

Like What?

I sit here empty-headed
Trying to find inspiration
I'm sitting in a crowd
Drinking tea
Listening to the chatter
But still I'm empty-headed
I look across the room
Ask a woman for a title
Title for my poem
Like what?
Was the reply
So here is my poem
And it's called like what
I sit here empty-headed

29 September 1998

Goodness and Badness

We are all basically good people
We need a bit of badness
Or the good becomes meaningless.
I wouldn't do anybody any harm
But my mean streak
Can make me sound wicked and mean.
We all have good and bad in us
It's the old story
Eventually good comes out on top
If you're bad through and through
Something's wrong!
Nobody's good through and through
If they were
If everybody was
How meaningless life would become.
We are all basically good people
We need a bit of badness
Or the good becomes nothing.

Goodness and badness
And a million bits in between.

1 October 1998

Just Talking

I was talking with a friend tonight
This 'n' that
Just talking.
I spoke of my breakdowns
Described how I shone
Talked deep and chattered to everyone
On a buzz
Could not sleep for days.
The friend said
What
Like speed!
I've never taken speed.
We were talking
This 'n' that
Just talking.
We decided my breakdowns
Are like taking speed
Likely the reason
I think so many pop/indie songs are about me
Drugs inspire many pop stars
I thought I was on my own.
I was talking with a friend tonight
This 'n' that
Just talking.

2 November 1998

Inspiration

When I'm ill
High as a kite
Middle of a breakdown
I'm inspired to write.
When I'm depressed

Deep and moody
I'm also inspired.
When I'm all right
Feeling not much at all
I lack inspiration.
When I'm ill
Having a breakdown
I'm inspired

20 January 1999

Windowsill

I sat upon the windowsill
A scarlet pigeon
Shat upon the fireman
On this cold winter's day.
I sat upon the windowsill
I could hear from afar
A drum roll
A banjo
However my feet did not tap.
I sat upon the window sill
Night came down
The light bulb blossomed
The wind did not
                    neglect the windmill.
I sat upon the windowsill
No No!!
I never did
Sit upon the windowsill.

11 February 1999

Deep Within

Deep within your mind
Deep within your soul
Cast away any thoughts
Cast away any feelings
When you find your innermost depths
There is nothing

Deep within your mind
Deep within your soul
What does it add up to?
Mostly nothing at all
You may have many thoughts
Many feelings
When you find your innermost depths
It adds up to nothing
Deep within your mind
Deep within your soul
Deep within

15 February 1999

My Farmhouse (Part Two)

The year is 1993, I'm working and living in Kettering. I'm getting stressed out with work, heading for a breakdown; I'm 32 years old, the lads I'm lodging with pull my leg, saying – 'Jesus became famous at 32.' Why? They don't know about my illness (I think?).

My breakdown is upon me, my small obsession with my dream farmhouse escalates, I start driving my car there. One night I knocked on the door; there was a young couple living there, the stars were shining. He didn't seem surprised to see me, we exchanged a few words and I went on my way. It was a big mystery to me who the house actually belonged to.

Christmas 1997: yet another breakdown, but I'm getting older and wiser. I'm renting a flat through an estate agent in Corby; I'm on friendly terms with them. My mind on a buzz, I asked them if they knew anything about the farmhouse; to my surprise they did. They told me who owned it and where to rent it from, they thought I was nuts – we had a laugh and a joke. Anyhow I looked in the phone book, and there was this bloke's number, so of course I phoned him. He seemed pretty annoyed, but once he realised I was harmless he calmed down a bit.

I've got to be honest: now that a lot of the mystery has gone, I'm not so obsessed with it. Even if I got six numbers on the lottery I would think twice. I still sometimes kid myself that the house was especially done up for me – but that's my illness.

Illness or no illness, we all need dreams – some dreams fade with time, just fade…

My farmhouse!!!

31 March 1999

Unhappy

I have a motor car
I have a big music collection
I love my music
I have a nice home
I should be happy
I'm not happy
I don't know why?
I have a motor car
I have a big music collection
I go out
I have friends
But I'm not happy
What's wrong with me?
I should be happy
I'm not
Why?
What makes people happy?
I don't know
I'm just an unhappy
Miserable old bugger
Unhappy!
Only joking
Hee! Hee!

28 April 1999

Ain't That a Shame

The world is spinning
We're still here!
Last Sunday was supposed to be the end
Did you hold your breath?
A brief thunderstorm
A bolt of lightning

The world is spinning
We're still here!
Some say they got the dates wrong
Personally I think
Some have nothing better to do
The doom and gloom merchants.
The world is spinning
We're still here!
A thunderstorm
A drop of rain
What's the game?
Ain't that a shame.

7 July 1999

Fish 'n' Chips

I sit here
Looking out the window
Nothing better to do
My mind is a blank
Is it today?
It doesn't look like it
I'm talking about the end
The millennium is near
Maybe the bug will do it?
Man relies on chips!
Computer chips
Not fish 'n' chips
I sit here
Looking out the window
Nothing better to do
I think of you
Ain't I a fool

14 July 1999

Nothing

I've decided to write about nothing
I should be able to write loads
Loads of nothing
My life adds up to nothing
My mind is full of nothing
I have all the creature comforts
A big music collection
A telly licence
I'm not in debt
But most of all I have nothing
It all adds up to nothing
I've decided to write about nothing
I bang my head off the wall
Pace up and down
Waiting for tomorrow
Tomorrow more of nothing
I've decided to write about…

4 August 1999

Dead Roses

Petals lay at my feet
Petals from a rose
A red rose
A yellow rose
Red roses are a symbol of love
Yellow roses are a symbol of friendship
The roses are dead
The petals lay at my feet
The girl
The love
The friendship
All of these are long gone
Petals lay at my feet
Petals from a rose
They lay upon the grave

The grave of my grandparents
The roses may be dead
But my love will live for ever
Dead roses

4 August 1999

Eclipse 1999

Was it worth the wait?
The big build-up
Did the earth move?
I wouldn't have noticed
A trip to Cornwall
It all went dark!
Not here
They said don't look!
We're still here
It didn't all end
Patrick Moore didn't smile
When does he?
Disappointed to say the least
Did you notice?
Two to three minutes
Did the earth move?
Was it worth the wait?

11 August 1998

Every Now and Then

Every now and then
Two to three weeks of torment
My body tells me I need it!
Sex, love, bodily contact.
Every now and then
Two to three months of calm and peace
My hormones calm down
Happy being on my own.
Every now and then

I climb the walls
Scream and pull out my hair
Two, maybe three weeks of torment
Every now and then.

12 August 1999

The Prisoner

Who is Number One?
You are Number Six
I am not a number
I am a free person
You are Number Two
Who is Number One?
After all is said and done
We are all Number One
Number One to ourselves
Who is Number One?
You are
You fool

18 August 1999

One Man Clapping

A trip to Cambridge
The Corn Exchange
Echo and the Bunnymen
1997 Evergreen tour
Sold out
Hundreds of people
Cheering clapping yelling
Pushed my way to the front
Some decent photos
Do the crowd hear what I hear?
McCulloch's lyrics
Cut through my soul
It should be me
One man clapping

I'm frozen on another planet
A trip to Cambridge
Evergreen tour
Mac's done it again

23 August 1999

The Raging Sea

The wind blows
I huff and puff
Crash against your bow
Up 'n' down
Like a steam ship
Like the raging sea
You are a mermaid
Jumping 'n' swimming
From wave to wave
The wind blows
We huff and puff
Scream 'n' shout
In 'n' out
Huff 'n' puff
Washed up
In love
On an empty beach
Waiting for the sea
The raging sea
The raging sea of love

21 September 1999

Exit the Thunderbird

The band have finished
A cheer from the crowd
A few boos
The DJ spins the wax
Time to go
Sober as a judge

I'm driving you see
Jacket on
Bye to a few friends
Dodge the dancers
Through the first doors
Pick up some flyers
Trip to the toilet
Through the main doors
The cold night air hits you like a tonic
People at the burger van
Key in the door
Key in the ignition
Bye bye Thunderbird

9 September 1999

Exit the Thunderbird (Take Two)

The band wasn't very good
Too many cover versions
What do you expect?
It is a 1950s R 'n' R Club
Jacket on I'm off!
Dodge the dancers
Too many old people
Hey I'm forty next year!
Not so young myself
See you in a fortnight my friend
Pick up some flyers
The night air is cool and refreshing
Open the door
Off I go!!!
Back to Corby

9 September 1999

Up

I've been down
Down and out

Pissed everybody about
I've been down
Down and out
Out of my box
Kicked the dog
I've been down
Down and out
I think I'll shout
Have a pint of stout
I've been down
Down and out
Why is this poem called 'Up'?

22 September 1999

Wrapper

Slowly I peel the wrapper off
My mouth wet with anticipation
Slowly I peel the wrapper off
Whisper sweet nothings
Slowly I peel the wrapper off
Wow nothing quite like it!
Slowly I peel the wrapper off
Slowly oh so very slowly

22 September 1999

Soul Sell

Why do you sell your soul?
You write song after song
Songs from your soul
Then you write songs complaining
About selling your soul
I write poems
Poems from my soul
At least you get recognition
Recognition and lots of money
Why do you sell your soul?

I'll tell you why!
We get off on it
Seeing peoples reaction
Why do you sell your soul?
Song after song
It helps people discover their soul
Soul sell! Soul sell!
Stop complaining
You're a pop star
Me I'm nothing
Soul sell
Soul

22 September 1999

Crumpled Paper

I sit down to write
I have to write
I have to let you know
I sit down to write
To write a letter
A letter of goodbye
The wording has to be right
No room for mistakes
Am I angry?
Am I sad?
I sit down to write
I have to let you know
It's not that I don't like you
It's not that I don't love you
You drive me insane
We're really not going anywhere
I sit down to write
I have to write
I have to let you know
One in the bin
Two in the bin
Ten in the bin
Crumpled paper
I have to let you know

I have to write
This letter of goodbye
Crumpled paper

9 October 1999

The Proverbial Spider

I put the kettle on
For my last cup of tea
I do it every night
Midnight!
Turn out the lights
Bedside light on
Undress
Make a roll-up
Bloody hell!
A spider
Is it the proverbial spider
Or just any old spider?
On go the lights
It's in my bed
The bloody spider
The proverbial spider

9 October 1999

Christmas

Christmas
Christmas time again!
Time to remember old friends
Time to spend money
It comes so quickly these days
The children excited in anticipation
Christmas
Christmas time again!
Feeling left out
Depressed and suicidal
The dark nights

No money
Christmas
Christmas time again!
Time to celebrate the birth of Christ
Time to get drunk
It comes and it's gone
Christmas
Christmas time again!

27 October 1999

Who am I?!!

1980 – 'Saturn Five', losing my virginity. 'The Mirror', also 1980, not knowing my father. Through my Jesus years – 'The Dawn of the New Tomorrow', then working out the fact that I am not Jesus; Ian McCulloch, my very own personal Jesus – I was, I am, greatly inspired by Echo and the Bunnymen! Sex, the lack of sex, love, marriage, divorce, my son Luke, the last 20 years of the 20th Century – I debate the fact that I am a poet; really it's a diary of my thoughts, feelings and observations, twisted with the fact that I'm a diagnosed schizophrenic – I am a product of the 20th Century, make of it what you will.

Thanks goes to my friends, family, and more recently Roger at the Hazelwood Bungalow in Corby; see you all after the millennium if we're still here?

4 November 1999

I.vi

The New Millennium, 1999–2000

What Next?

Sit down young man
And how are you today?
I look up
I look down
You know
OK I suppose
How is your sex life?
Bloody hell straight to the point
Frustrating
Non-existent
I look up
I look down
It's not sex I'm after
It's TLC, love, friendship
Thought of a prostitute?
I look up
Bloody hell
Where's he coming from?
Where does he get off!
I look down
I keep looking down
See you in three months
Time to go?
It's only been four-and-a-half minutes
I look up
Look down
I keep looking down
I leave the surgery
A bloody prostitute
What next!!!

10 November 1999

Food

I need food
Food for thought
'Coz I can't think of a thing
With the title, 'Food'
Give me food
Food for thought
But food
I mean
Food for a title
I need food
Food for thought
Food

17 November 1999

The New Millennium

They say life begins at forty
I'm forty next year
The New Millennium
Two Thousand
A new love?
I've forgotten what love is
To put yourself second
The New Millennium
Two Thousand
Will man ever stop fighting?
Help one another
Love one another
Unfortunately I'm not that optimistic
The New Millennium
Two Thousand
The second coming
Is He here?
What could He do anyway?!!
Two thousand
Two thousand and one

Two thousand and two
Don't let me grow old
Old and lonely
We all need love
They say life begins at forty
I'm forty next year
The new millennium

18 November 1999

One of Us

She smiles
Smiles laughs and jokes
An occasional flirt
It won't be the same
She smiles
Smiles, laughs and jokes
Joins in
Almost one of us
Down to earth
It won't be the same
Soon to part
A friend to everyone
Sometimes a pot of tea
She smiles
Smiles, laughs and jokes
One of us
Unfortunately no more
One of us

18 November 1999

Christmas Eve

Adam was in the garden
Wandering about
Bored
If only I had someone to talk to
Hands behind his back

Kicking stones
Christmas hadn't been invented
Jesus Christ wasn't even thought of
God looked down upon Adam
And said
I know I'll give him a mate
Someone to talk to
Make love and all that stuff
So it was
God created Eve
A mate for Adam
Adam must have thought it was Christmas
But because Christmas hadn't been invented
We'll just call her Eve
Christmas Eve

1 December 1999

Inspiration #2

You don't need inspiration
To be in love
You don't need inspiration
To be heartbroken
It just happens
But you need inspiration
To write a poem
Even a crap poem
Inspiration

8 December 1999

Who Are They?

They watch you
They push you
They promise the world
They give you dreams
They guide you
They turn out the lights

They blind you
Who are they?
Why me?
They watch me
They push me
The price is high
Have I met them?
Television
Radio
Pop songs
They watch me
Waiting for my next move
I'm waiting for them
They watch you
They push you
They promise the world

19 December 1999

1-1-2000

January the first 2000
I feel alive
Not jumping for joy
But alive
A fresh start
Maybe a new love?
Time to look forward
Not back
Forget the past
The twentieth century wasn't all bad
Some happy times
Some great times
January the first 2000
I feel alive

1 January 2000

Barrel of Dreams

I live in a barrel
A barrel of forgotten dreams
That used to spin around and around
Past the wonderful mysterious mystical moon
Nowhere nothing
Was too small too big or untouchable.
I live in a barrel
A barrel of dreams
Tossed up, down
Pushed and pulled
Up hill, down hill.
The barrel has lost its magic
It isn't broken
It just seems to be stuck
Somewhere down the hill.
I live in a barrel
How I remember those days
Spinning in outer space
High up the hill
In my barrel
Barrel of dreams.

20 January 2000

Going Nowhere Slow

Going nowhere
Going nowhere slow
So slow it hurts
So slow it's painful
The clock on the wall
Tick tock
Night after night
Chimes my life away
Slowly oh so very slowly
Nothing to do
Nowhere to go

No one to share the empty hours
Going nowhere
Going nowhere slow
So slow it hurts
So slow it's painful

25 February 2000

Everything to Share

I have everything
Everything to share
The one thing I don't have
Is the one to share it with
I go places
But I don't even try to find that person
I have given up on myself
I feel so low
The girl that could change everything
I have so much
So much to give
I know she's out there
Unfortunately she has to find me
I'm not holding my breath
I do dream
I have everything
Everything to share

27 February 2000

Here She Comes

Here she comes
Walking down the way
She always makes my day
Smiling, laughing
Nothing gets her down
She is the sunshine
The sunshine in my life
Nothing is too much

What I would do for her
Here she comes
Walking down the way
And she's coming to stay
Sweet sixteen
I pray it's not to late
For me her Dad
To put some sunshine her way
Here she comes
Walking down the way
Natalie is here to stay
The sunshine of my day

11 March 2000

Home

My flat used to be my home
My flat still is my home
But my home has been invaded
Invaded by S Club 7, Five, Boyzone, Geri
Need I go on!
I used to sit there deep and in solitude
Echo and the Bunnymen, Jesus and Mary Chain
Happy in my depression
My flat used to be my home
My flat still is my home
Nowadays my feet tap
Nowadays I smile
To the up-beat of the Spice Girls
Come back Echo…
Come back Mary Chain!
I like being miserable
But most of all
I like my daughter's company
She's a real live wire
My flat used to be my home

22 March 2000

Colours

Black and white
Some see only black and white
Colours
Life has many colours and shades
The black dark storm cloud
May have a bright colourful rainbow
Not much actually is black and white
All right a chess table
But the game isn't B/W
A bit like life
Full of different moves
Full of colour
Full of different ideas
Black and white
Many spiralling colours
Truth is stranger than fiction
You may think it's red!
You may think it's blue!
It could be pink?
It could be purple?
Colours
Colours in the dark
Colours in the light
Colours!

22 March 2000

Spinning Thoughts

When did I find myself
When did my head stop spinning?
Was it yesterday
Maybe a few years ago
My head, mind, inner thoughts
Used to spin and spin
Breakdown after breakdown.
When did I find myself

When did my head stop spinning?
I'm afraid of a future breakdown
Because my last breakdown
There was nothing to spin
But I had the pain of spinning.
When did I find myself
When did my head stop spinning?
I have lost the competing thoughts
More happy and content
Was it yesterday?
No, a few years ago
Spinning thoughts.

31 March 2000

My Car Keys

Walking down the stairs
In my first-floor flat
Opening the door
Keys on my mind
Mustn't forget
I'd be locked out
Walking to my car
In the car park
Opening the door
Keys in my hand
Mustn't forget
Always remember
My car keys
Walking down the stairs
Walking to my car

1 May 2000

Confederate

When I was ill early on
I used to break words up
Breaking words up meant so much to me

Benson and Hedges translated to
Buddy Holly
Bill Haley
Very mixed up but it meant something
What I don't know now
USA
You Suck Another
Confederate
Rockabilly rhythms going through my head
CON – life is a con
FED – being fed bullshit by the media
DER – you are stupid
ATE – I can't remember
I was ill
It really meant something at the time
God knows what now

10 May 2000

Don't Fade Away

I used to dream all the time
My dreams are dead
Died a slow boring agonising death
Some, even most, have come true
A nice home
A decent motor car
Decent money without working
A large music collection
Every now and then
I find it hard to appreciate
What I have
What I have built up
But most of all
I have lost the dreamer in me
I seem to be standing still
I can't see the horizon
Because I'm standing on it
Walking over and beyond
I don't wish to be sixteen again
I just wish?

I don't know what I wish
I haven't a dream
I used to dream all the time
My dreams have died
Fame and fortune with my poems
A prosperous marriage
World peace
My dreams are dead
Just faded away
Don't fade away!

19 May 2000

Stacey

My daughter has a sister
Her name is Stacey
I'm not Stacey's father
Stacey misses her dad
'Coz she's a bit bad
Smoking at fourteen
Drunk last night
No solid family life
My daughter has a sister
I'm not her dad
Stacey is a rebel
She's only fourteen
Time to change, mature
My daughter has a sister
Her name is Stacey
Crazy Stacey!

21 May 2000

Why?

Why do you smoke?
Ten a day now
Twenty a day soon

Why do you smoke?
Four pounds and rising
They'll never come down
Why do you smoke?
To be one of the gang
Nicotine it's great!
Why do you smoke?
Breath like an ashtray
A social leper
Why do you smoke?
Because people tell me not to
To get up your nose
Why do you smoke?
Why? Why? Why?

24 May 2000

Who Am I?

Who am I?
Why am I here?
I look in the mirror
I look deep into my own eyes
I can see sadness, frustration
I need to communicate
Communicate with others
Tell them
Let them know
Things they probably already know
Somehow it needs to come from me
Why?
Who am I?
Why am I here?
I look at you
I look deep into your eyes
I smash all the mirrors
The mirrors that show me myself
I need to communicate
Communicate with myself
I need to find myself

I need my father
The one who was never there
Who am I?
Why am I here?
I almost resent my mother
Just for being my mother
I look at her
I look at myself
I look at you
Who am I?
Why am I here?

31 May 2000

Close That Door

Don't do this
Don't do that
Close that door
Keep off the grass
No smoking
Can you whistle?
You can't sing
Don't do this
Don't do that
Like this?
No!
Like this
Don't do that
Don't do this
Close that door
Thank you!

31 May 2000

The Look

Have you the conviction?
Have you the look?

I sometimes have that look
I've been there so many times
I'm looking for answers
Have you been there?
Have you seen the mystery?
The more you see
The less you really know
I don't need psychedelic drugs
I have schizophrenia
I've been there
Deep within
Far in outer space
Have you that look?
It does fade
Slips through your fingers
Like grains of sand
Have you the conviction?
Have you the look?

5 June 2000

Holiday in the Sun

When you go on holiday
Where do you go?
I'd like to get away
Far far away.
When you go on holiday
Where do you go?
What I'd really like
Is a holiday away from myself.
When you go on holiday
Where do you go?
Nowhere
Nowhere at all
Because there I am!
Holiday in the sun.

21 June 2000

First Impressions

Here he is
We've waited months
Nine months
A fragile baby boy
My boy
Our boy
Ten little toes
Ten little fingers
I'm excited and calm all at the same time
Nurse
Is his head all right?
It seems to be swollen
Yes yes that's normal
My wife is absolutely knackered
Well of course
I hold my son
Wrapped in his little sheet
I look deeply
Lovingly
Into his eyes
I quietly talk
I can't stop talking
Letting him know
I am here
His father
Wow!
He's fantastic
Here he is
We've waited months
Nine months

28 June 2000

Planet Earth

The earth
Millions of years old

How did it all begin
What came first
The chicken or the egg?
People, humans
Where did we come from?
If we came from another planet
Where did that planet come from?
The earth
Millions of years old
Nobody knows
Evolution
God, faith, Christianity
Who knows?
The chicken or the egg?
Millions of questions
We might never know
The earth
Millions of years old
Millions of years to come
My life
Your life
Just an insignificant speck
On this planet
Planet earth.

20 July 2000

The House

I went for a walk today
Across the fields
At Great Oakley.
I thought I'd forgotten,
Put my farmhouse outta my mind
But there it was
The house
The dream
In all its splendour.
I went for a walk
It brought back old memories
I'll never have the money

That was part of the dream too
That much I've lost
But there it was
The house
The dream.
I tell myself
It's just a farmhouse
But no it's not
It's part of me
Part of my life.
I went for a walk
Across the fields
The feelings I get
Are empty feelings?
Just empty.

25 July 2000

Uneasy

I'm sitting in the club
Downstairs from the band
I feel a bit uneasy
It's not my usual gig or scene
I'm scared to look up
I'm uneasy
I'm staring
Staring into my pint
Has the band started?
I can't wait to move
Fiver on the door
Four big black men
Security just for me, I jest
Posters in the hall
Vandalised with swastikas
Get the picture
Skinheads
A skinhead club
Not my normal scene
Time to go?
I can't wait to leave

Psychobillies are crazy
Psychobilly is my scene
But skinheads
Fuck that
Goodnight!

26 July 2000

The Chocolate Doughnut

There she was
Sitting on her bed
Her back facing the door
Her hand moves quickly
Secretively
She thinks I haven't noticed
A few hours later, I say
Enjoy the doughnut
She's lost for words
Days, weeks
Have passed since that day
I feel guilty now
She can't pass McDonald's
Without buying me one
Her guilt has turned to love
She buys me one all the time
My daughter
And the
Chocolate doughnut!

26 July 2000

Here I Go!?

Here I go!?
Here I go again
Climbing the ladder
Faster and faster
Escalating up the pyramid
Slow and mysterious to start

Then it takes a grip
I know it's wrong
I know I'm hallucinating
Here I go!
Here I go again
Two maybe three rungs up the ladder
Your feet leave the ground
It doesn't matter any more
It doesn't matter you're hallucinating
Here I go
Here I go again
Hospital
All those pretty young nurses
Pushing you higher
Important people, psychiatrists
Pushing you higher
Here I go!!!
Here I go again
I'm important
Very important

2 August 2000

Jesus in the Eighties

The closing of the twentieth century
A poem here
A poem there
In and out of hospital
Deluded I was the one
The chosen one
The eighties and the nineties
Sign after sign
Showing me the way
They never came for me
They never did
The end of the twentieth century
I had some fun
Not all fun
Week after week
Waiting for the money

Pumped full of drugs
The eighties and nineties
Deep down, I knew
I knew
It wasn't me
If I had have made it
I'd just be another forgotten popstar, poet
Jesus in the eighties!

11 August 2000

First Breakdown – 1980

The Kenny Everett TV show
Sex with Jamie when I was younger
Leaving school – college
Growing up – not growing up
Looking for love with girls
Looking for sex with girls
Rockabilly rhythms
Rockabilly song lyrics
Money – spot the ball
First experience of sex with a girl
Not knowing a thing about the Bible –
And saying I could write a modern one,
Thinking anybody could be Jesus –
But I didn't think it was me –
That came later
The world was at my feet –
But I didn't have the money.
The odd pop song –
Kate Bush – 'The Man with the Child in His Eyes'
Not understanding girls, love, relationships –
No one to talk to about it
Not knowing my father
But most of all –
The Kenny Everett TV show!!!

15 August 2000

Gay

Are you gay?
Are you a homosexual?
You say you're not on that bus
You say you like your pussy
How do you know?
Have you tried it?
They say you should try everything once!
Are you gay?
Are you a homosexual?
You don't know!
I know I'm not gay
I know I'm not homosexual
You see
I've been down that road
Does it scare you?
I'm not afraid
Are you gay?
Are you a homosexual?

20 August 2000

Pay Day

I don't work
I don't need to work
I've won the lottery
The DSS lottery.
Many years ago
I was diagnosed…
I've hit the big time
No third degree
Down the dole office
I stroll down the post office
Here he comes
Start counting the money
I don't work
I don't need to work

Yee-ha!!!
Pay day.

23 August 2000

Soap Operas

Soap operas
What a load of crap
Get a life
Soap operas
Hypnotising the masses
Into their way of thinking
Soap operas
While the gossips are talking
About some fictional character
They're leaving some other poor fucker alone!
Soap operas
Get a life!

23 August 2000

I Need It

I need it
Once a fortnight
Do I need it
They say I need it
I believe I need it
Life wouldn't be the same without it
It helps me sleep
Slows me down
I'm a skyrocket without it
I need it
Once a fortnight
I look forward to it
I'm a junky
A prescription junky
Give me the drugs!
The syringe that penetrates my skin
I need it

Oh yes I need it
My fortnightly fix
A couple of tablets
Side-effect tablets
I need it
The needle that penetrates my buttocks
I need it
The medication that keeps me sane
Helps me sleep
Slows me down
I need it
Schizophrenic
No, I'm not schizophrenic
I have my needle

27 September 2000

Why? #2

Why do I write?
Why did I write?
Losing my virginity
Inspiration!
Why do I write?
Trying to express myself
Deep from within
Mostly from depression
But not always
Why write
Trying to communicate
Why?
A diary!
A diary of thoughts and feelings
Some good
Some crap
Why do I write?
I don't know
I really don't
Why?

25 October 2000

Where Is She?

Where is she?
I'm here
Where is she?
At home
Feet up
I'm here
Seven carrier bags
Some light
Some heavy
Where is she?
The woman
The woman of my dreams
I'm here
Doing the shopping
Loaded down
My daughter
At home
Maybe school
Where is she?
The woman of my dreams
Anyhow!
The woman of my dreams
Wouldn't be doing the shopping
Where is she?
In my bed
No!
Where is she?

25 October 2000

The Launderette

I don't need the launderette
I have a washing machine
A washing machine from the catalogue
Ten bob a week
I don't need the launderette

I have a tumble dryer
A tumble dryer from the catalogue
Ten bob a week
Launderette?
I don't need the launderette
Ten bob a week
The catalogue fixed me up
P.S.
Why was the washing machine laughing?
'Coz it took the piss out the knickers.

20 September 2000

I.vii

2000–2002

Question

How would you ask?
Nice
Nasty
Funny
Sexy
Shy
The question is
Are you gay?
Nice
Nasty
Funny
Sexy
Shy
Well?

1 November 2000

Treading on Eggshells

Always moody
Treading on eggshells
There's a sadness with his anger
A man of leisure
The dole made him work
Moody with his mother
My best mate
We don't see each other any more
I've tried

He broke my heart
Best mates for years
Moody angry sad
Did we understand one another?
Maybe we didn't
Always moody
Treading on eggshells

12 November 2000

Oxygen to the Soul

My brain needs oxygen
My brain needs nicotine
My soul needs inspiration
My soul needs a twist
A twist to write this poem
Without oxygen
I wouldn't have a brain
Without oxygen
I wouldn't have a soul
I take a deep breath
For inspiration
For oxygen
For nicotine
Oxygen to the soul

20 November 2000

Reminiscing

I'm not happy with today
I'm less happy with tomorrow
Yesterday?
I know about yesterday
When I fall in love
I know it will end
I can't wait
So I can remember
Look at the photos

Today is wet cement
The past is concrete
I'm always looking back
Not just love
Life
Good or bad
Reminiscing

29 November 2000

Why the Long Face?

She sits in the corner
With nothing
Nothing but a long face
She opens her mouth
And rubbish comes out
She sits in the corner
Very rarely
A kind word
She sits in the corner
Hiding behind those shades
Insensitive
Insensitive isn't the word
It comes off the top of her head
She thinks it's right
She thinks it's the gospel
Because she says so
She sits in the corner
With nothing
Nothing but a long face

30 November 2000

Gone

If you don't stay tonight
I'll be gone in the morning
You didn't stay
And I was gone

I wasn't sure where you were
At your mum's?
In the arms of that bloke?
The end
After just two years of
Till death do us part
Our baby boy
Growing up calling *him* Dad
It makes me sad
If only this
If only that
You didn't stay
And I was gone

4 December 2000

Them and Us

You fancy me
You think I fancy you
I'm having a laugh
I'm bored
Passing the time
Maybe I do fancy you
I hadn't thought about it
That's all you think about
That's all you think I think about
She's a bit of all right
Only joking
No you're not
I give up
Social workers
Service users
I give up

4 December 2000

Julia

Here she is
The woman

The voice
The lady on the phone
I've talked and talked
When I'm up
When I'm down
Usually down
The soft gentle voice
Reassuring
Picking me up
Here she is
The woman
The voice
A mystery no more
Here she is
Nice to meet you
I mustn't moan
We're not on the phone

6 December 2000

The Monster

I sit here
Wondering
When how where
If
If at all
Feeling
Feeling the future
I feel fine
It's not gone
It's not left me
But I feel fine
I sit here
When how where
Have I outgrown it
It's there
It's still there
I sit here
Wondering
Wandering through

The wardrobe of my mind
I sit here

13 January 2001

Ice Cold

Ice cold
Ice cold spider's web
Frozen in time
Skating on thin ice
Ice cold
Ice cold has my fist
The fist to thump him, them
Them that did it
Did it again
To my car
Ice cold
Ice cold feelings
From him, to me, to my motor
Ice cold

14 February 2001

Great Balls of Fire

I'm on fire
My chest is burning
My head is spinning
I'll never find another
Sex?
Great sex
One pill
Two pills
I wanna die
I'm on fire
Burning from head to toe
She's gone
My fault
Her fault

Nobody's fault
I'm on fire
Call 999
Ambulance
No
The fire brigade
I'm on fire
Stress
I'll tell you about stress
Burning from the inside out
Fire
I'm on fire
Great balls of fire!!!

21 March 2001

Great Buckets of Water

You are pathetic
Calm down
It's only a girl
Plenty more fish in the sea
Stress?
Calm down
Take some deep breaths
Grow up
Get a grip
Great buckets of water!

21 March 2001

Nappy

Nappy nappy
Baby's bum
Nappy nappy
I'm so happy
Big boy now
Goodbye nappy
Shitty nappy

Nappy nappy
Long gone
Nappy

9 May 2001

Straitjacket

I wish I wish
I still had it!
My drape jacket
Velvet collar and cuffs
I wish I wish
I never gave it away
Trying to impress
Young lady
Didn't work
She took it!
Said thanks
I wish I wish
I still had it!
My drape jacket
Straitjacket
No no
Drape jacket

9 May 2001

Protest Poem

I sit here
Trying to write a poem
A protest poem
Problem is
I haven't a protest in me
I don't watch telly
I don't see the news
What if nobody protested?
Does it make a difference
Or just give the police something to do?

So I sit here
Am I boring?
I most likely am
I don't like drunks
That's no protest
I sit here
Trying to write a poem
A protest poem

15 May 2001

I'm So Happy!

I'm moody
Moody and miserable
Shouting and moaning
At my poor darling daughter
Stop stop
I'm sorry
Five minutes and I'm doing it again
Stop stop
Empty the ashtrays
Tidy round
Just little things
I'm happy
I'm so happy
Relax
Turn off the PC
Take some deep breaths
I'm happy
Really I'm miserable
Miserable and moody
No, happy
I'm so happy!!!

16 May 2001

Orange

Orange is a colour!
It's not red

It's not yellow
Orange is a fruit!
It's not an apple
It's not a banana
Orange is bright
Orange is cheerful
Orange is a phone company
Orange!!!

30 May 2001

Blighty

Me I'm English
Me I'm British
Proud of the language
You don't talk American
You don't talk Australian
You talk English
Me I'm English
Me I'm British
I don't work
I'm disabled
I'm looked after
Looked after with money
Where would I be
Schizophrenic in Iraq?
Me I'm English
Me I'm British
Thank God for Blighty!!!
Good old Blighty!

30 May 2001

Election 2001

Elect me!
Don't vote for him!
Vote for me
What can you do for me?

What can you do for the country?
Promises promises
Why vote for him?
Why vote for you?
Foot and mouth?
You all have your feet in your mouths
Pie in the sky
Promises promises
Don't vote for him!
Vote for me
I think I'll stay in my bed!
Sleeping tax?
OK I'll get up
Use your vote
Why?
Election 2001
Goodnight!

6 June 2001

It Never Crossed My Mind

I used to believe I was Jesus
It never crossed my mind
Jesus was the Son of God
Of course I knew he was
I was never the Son of God!
My delusion
Where did it come from?
I mean God as my Dad
Recently I was told
God is Jesus
God the Father
God the Son
God the Holy Spirit
Well, I was never a God!
It never crossed my mind

5 July 2001

Have You Seen the Light?

Have you seen the light?
The light does not shine
In many of our lives
Many don't bother
I'm a good boy!
I'm a good girl!
I'm going to heaven
Being good alone
Doesn't lead to heaven
Have you seen the light?
For Jesus
And Jesus alone
Is the light!
The light of everlasting life

6 September 2001

Move Over Rover

It comes to us all
Different people
Different times
There is a time in your life
Time to move
Move over Rover
Your time has gone!
The young move up
You're not the bee's knees any more
Your day has passed!
The kids aren't kids any more
Time to move
The wit is not yours
The young with their new outlook!
It comes to us all
Move over Rover
You old fart
Move over

12 September 2001

Two Minutes

Eternity before you're born
Eternity after you die
Your life?
Two minutes and it's gone!

27 September 2001

Walking with Jesus

She has that smile
She has that look
Happy and content
Not looking over her shoulder
Always looking forward
A prayer here!
A prayer there!
A prayer for you and me
God is in her heart
Jesus is her best friend
She is full of life
She is full of joy
Praise to the Lord!
For if you knew of my daughter's joy
You yourself would seek the Lord
I may not be a Christian
I may not understand
But my daughter
Really is…
Walking with Jesus

28 September 2001

Five Years

Five years?
What do you want?

Where do you see yourself?
Are you happy?
Yes I'm happy
Life's pretty good
A roof over my head
Food in the fridge
Five years?
I see myself…
Pretty much the same
That's not too much to ask?
Sex would be nice
But it's not everything
A publisher for my poems
Yes! Yes! But not likely
Five years, ten years…
Just leave me alone
My music, my motor, my home
Five years?
Just leave me alone

15 October 2001

Yesterday

The young girls
Down the street
Look in the mirror
Look at yourself
Am I sad?
No! No!
Just fat!
Teenager today?
No! No!
That's all yesterday…

16 October 2001

Not a Chance

Filling out the form
In the local charity shop

Some Voluntary work
Two-and-a-half hours a week
Sorting through the jumble
Last question on side one
Any health problems?
'No problems
But I am schizophrenic'
Didn't get to side two
Didn't get to my references
Didn't even see side two
Discrimination like this
What chance do we have?
Some chance!
Fat chance!
Not a chance...

30 November 2001

King of Kings

I was the King
The King of Kings
Well maybe the court jester
My diamonds were bells
My crown made of cloth
Sitting on my throne
With a disease or two
The disease of grandeur
The disease of deluding myself
The disease of schizophrenia
I was the King
The King of Kings

24 January 2002

Maybe Isn't Enough

We're all looking for love
Looking for that someone
You meet someone

You think to yourself
Maybe just maybe?
Maybe? Isn't enough

5 April 2002

She

She is sweet
She is soft
The taste you can't forget
You tell yourself
It's only sex
She's gone
It's all over
She is sweet
She is soft
She is Misery

5 April 2002

Six Months v Two Bottles of Cider

I smile at her
She smiles back
I say the odd word or two
A birthday kiss!
She sits in my motor
Away from the cold
Months and months
Am I getting anywhere?
I get the date!
Things are happening…
Along he comes with his two bottles of cider
Au revoir, cheerio
Why did I bother?

4 June 2002

Could It Be You?

The sun is shining
I'm sitting here
With nothing to do
Thinking of you!
I'm really quite blue
Because there is no you
'Thinking of you'
Is just a line in this poem
The sun is shining
I'm waiting for someone
Could it be you?
The sky is blue
I am too!

21 May 2002

'Women'

He's paying the mortgage
Problems seeing his kid!
She's taking him to the cleaners
This one's not in love
Two boys and a baby girl
Takes the shit day after day
I tell myself
I'm best on my own
Got off lightly once maybe twice
Walking through town today!
Many uglies walking by
There she was…
A couple arm-in-arm
She was perfect
The curves straight from heaven
That's it
That's why
'Women'

7 August 2002

Chimes

The clock chimes
Another hour of my life
Hours and hours
Doing nothing
Trying to fill the time
The clock chimes
Tick tock
Nearly time for bed!
All I do is sleep
Sleep away the boredom
The clock chimes
Hang on?!!!
No the clock doesn't chime
It needs a new battery
It gets its new battery
The clock chimes
And I sleep
Sleep away another day!
I'm not always this boring
Honestly!

15 September 2002

Then and Now

Six years old
Running for the bus
Me, Mum and Jamie
Jamie my older brother
Running to meet him
My Mum's new boyfriend
With all these men
I don't know whether I'm coming or going
But I'm only six
I don't know any different
Sharing my Mum's heartache

You can't rely on any man
I'm that man now!!!
Today's generations?
Good luck
You're going to need it!

8 November 2002

Guy Fawkes Night

You may have a friend?
You may have a lover?
Your lover should be everything
Your lover should be special
If it's just sex anybody will do!
You don't get any more intimate
Than sharing your body
Just a kiss?!!!
And it's November the fifth

8 November 2002

The Roots of Mental Illness

It could be in your childhood
It could be in your teens
I reckon it's all to do with love
It started for me before I was born
My father pissing off
It's always been a mystery
Puppy love is important
In my late teens
I had two big love affairs
No intercourse was involved
I made love with someone I wasn't in love with
And a couple of months later I went gaga
I remember I just wanted to be loved
And to love someone back
Instead I ended up like my father
I could be wrong?

But love
The root of just about all mental illness

9 November 2002

Same Old Song

I'm forty-two years old
Probably halfway through my life
Two teenage kids
One that I have not a lot to do with
The other quite a lot
But only recently.
They say life begins at forty
Me? I've always been a teenager
But when I catch my reflection in the shop window
I am fat and old
No teenager!
That's all yesterday
What do I want?
Where do I see myself at sixty maybe?
On the whole I'm quite happy
Happy being a bachelor sorry divorcee
But it was that long ago
I just consider myself as single
I don't feel as if I need to change
I don't know if I could change
If she is out there?
I'm willing to give it a go!
Apart from that I'll just keep plodding along
Humming the same old song.

9 November 2002

…And They All Lived Happily Ever After

Bollocks!

10 November 2002

I.vii

The Living End, 2003

Wrapping Paper

'Christmas'
What's it all about?
Wrapping paper!
You spend £5? £50? £500?
Without the paper it's nothing
Surprise! Surprise!
All under the tree…
Take away the wrapping
No suspense!
No surprise!
Christmas?
Yep!
Wrapping paper…

26 February 2003

Concrete and Imagination

You imagine some song's may be about you
You imagine the TV's talking at you
If you are this someone?
Where's the concrete? The proof!
After all this time
And you're still sitting there alone
You imagine you're someone
The reality is quite different
Concrete and imagination
No concrete!
Just loads of imagination…

2 May 2003

Bollocks

Bollocks!
The meaning of life…
Yes… Bollocks!
But you have to look a bit deeper
What makes the world go round?
OK… partly money
But why money…?
To attract the opposite sex!
Why do you do almost anything?
Why did I write this poem?
To just keep going…
The ultimate goal
To reproduce!
There's your answer…
Bollocks!
The meaning of life…
Just bollocks!

13 October 2003

This Jesus Guy

A few years back…
I had some silly weird thoughts!
I was this Jesus guy
But you have to ask yourself
What is his interpretation of Jesus?
Once you understand my interpretation…
Maybe I'm not so crazy
OK I'm no Christian!
A few years back…
I was in love with love
A daydream believer…
Nowadays!
Just bored…
Millennium come and gone
Well!

Where is He?
This Jesus guy…
Boring!

19 October 2003

Zero Out of 300

Why do you write?
Why did you start?
Why do you continue?
Something to do!
Pass a few minutes!
Why not!
Do you look within?
Do you know yourself?
Really… Why do you write?
Deep down… The real reason!
Why do we do anything!
Sex… To get laid!
Oh… What's your score?
That's easy
The title of this poem…

20 October 2003

Just a Dream

You spend your life buying records, CDs
All your favourites
You slip into this kind-a dream world
You become part of it!
'A rock 'n' roll monster'
You wouldn't harm a fly…
But they cart you off anyway!
Years in and out the funny farm!
You keep buying the music!
Fuelling the ego…
One day…
It all becomes pointless

You still have the records…
You still have the dream…
But no one's listening!

28 October 2003

Keep Walking

I walk by…
I walk round…
Most likely you…
Hey! I really don't know
Your ideas for me!
I do know mine for you
You are everything!
Maybe I don't know you?
The bit I think I know
Yes! You're everything!
I walk by…
I walk round…
Sometimes I can be a bit off!
That's part of the game
You can also be a bit off!
Is that the same game?
Walls and rules are there to suit!
I walk by…
I walk round…
Maybe I should just keep walking…

28 October 2003

Not Even a Has-been…

Bored to death…
Bored to the back teeth…
It's all nothing!
Some might say I've everything?
Take a young man!
Just moved in…
It's all new!

Everything to look forward to…
When you've been to Jupiter and back!
When you've been 'The Man'!
Yes, it may be called schizophrenia?
Just the same it happened!
Everything becomes an anticlimax
Boredom has a whole new meaning
You become a prisoner of your own memories
You're easily a bit of a joke!
Yes!!!
Bored to death…
Bored to the back teeth…
It's all nothing
Do something!
Go back to college?
You didn't hear a thing…
Argh… schizophrenia?
As I said
You didn't hear a thing!

30 October 2003

It's Huge!!!

I have a massive?
Wait for it…
Music collection!!!
Subconsciously collected to attract females
Which when they see it!
It is so massive!
They just walk away!
Who can blame them?
IT'S HUGE!!!

1 November 2003

Maybe Tomorrow?

No matter how fed up I get!
No matter how bored…

Depressed or Manic!!!
It's always in my mind –
Maybe tomorrow?
What is it that's out there?
Six numbers on the Lotto?
Being discovered as this Jesus guy?
A fantastic poet?
I can almost touch it!
I bang my head from wall to wall…
Deep down I am an optimist!
Maybe it's to love and to be loved?
I will just have to wait
Until tomorrow!
Maybe tomorrow?

4 November 2003

Sitting on the Fence

You may discuss your views
Argue your point!
See both sides?
You get to the point
You just don't have an argument
You may think you do?
Look again!
Look and listen?
You may very well disagree
Later… by yourself
There just isn't an argument
And that's with nearly everything…
In your own mind
Think of a discussion
And you'll see what I mean!

14 November 2003

Famous Madmen

Famous madmen
Pay cash for the illness

Some friends of mine
Pay hundreds
To be like me!!!
We all admire the famous
Tim Booth today?
Jim Morrison yesterday?
Famous madmen!
Famous because of mental illness
Some like myself 'just crazy'
Some have to buy the madness
When I write a poem
I can sometimes get some strange looks!
Maybe looked down on?
Tim and Jim, my two examples
Wouldn't even get in our little club!
'Hazelwood Bungalow'
They would be considered too mentally ill
Christ! Jim even o/d
Next time you're looking at me
Look again...

17 November 2003

The Donkey and the Carrot

She must know I've noticed her?!!!
Unfortunately she's already in a relationship
And even if she wasn't? Well...
I constantly tell myself
I can handle the situation
It's no big deal!
But there she is again!
In my mind...
And here's the poem...
'The Donkey and the Carrot'
Why that title?
Well...
I'm the donkey, she's the carrot...
Should I do this? Should I do that?
Confusing the poor donkey
Please tell...

In the story…
Did the donkey ever get his carrot?

17 November 2003

This Jesus Guy (An Interpretation)

How many people have an opinion about the Bible and its contents? Yet how many have actually read a single word in it? Let alone understand any of it! Well, I was one of those and quite honestly still to this day know and understand so little about 'the Word'

Here we go… apart from Sunday School, which I really don't remember, my first encounter with the Bible was in school. I must have been eleven years old. It was in the RE lesson; this girl asked me, along with many others, my opinion about God. I told her, 'God is an invention for people with not much in their lives, which means God is good because it gives these people something.' Remember, I was only eleven, very different from an eleven-year-old today, and that this notion was my very own. Note: when you say something out loud it can be so different from just thinking it.

Some years later, one of my lines when trying to get laid (and it worked) was that anybody, including myself, could write a new Bible because the old one was so out of date! Remember, I didn't know anything about the book!

Songs – pop songs, even crap ones had, and still do have, a big influence in my life. It was in my head that anybody could be 'the second coming', because of the hit single, Johnny Mathis, 'When A Child Is Born', which isn't so crazy – take a look at eighties pop culture, so many were self-appointed Messiahs, probably for that very same reason.

The big difference being – I was in hospital. 'This Jesus thing' I never did take seriously and that's the truth! I just got caught up in the eighties thing. Occasionally some of the other wackos in the hospitals would say or ask me if I was Jesus. The first time this happened, I lost it and trashed my room causing over £2,000 worth of damage. No doctor or anyone asked me why. In my illness this pushed me more manic because it logically seemed part of a conspiracy.

So what have we got? God is an invention, anybody could write a new Bible, Johnny Mathis inspired a whole generation of wannabe Gods, and contrary to popular belief, I never took the whole thing that seriously, but it did sometimes seem like a conspiracy that they wanted it to be me.

Just to finish, take a look at my music collection! Firstly I live out so many of the songs, it's so much more than just a noise! And then listen to where the songs take you!!! Then and only then tell me I'm crazy…

18 November 2003

What Is It?

What is my illness?
Where does it come from?
If I could get to the real secrets
Maybe I could prevent myself ever being ill again…
Maybe it is chemical?
Maybe hereditary?
When it happens
My whole nervous system turns upside down
When you're manic
Everything is larger than life!
Forget – the Jesus thing…
Forget – not knowing my father
The Kenny Everett TV show…
All that music rubbish!
The illness makes all that…
But what actually is it?

19 November 2003

I Am What I Am

'I am what I am'
You can't do much
Until you accept yourself…
When I stop trying to justify everything
Even my very existence
With all these poems…
I just might get somewhere?
Move on… Get a life…
Even sing the stupid song…
Hopefully?
Maybe?
This is it for now!
If you hear someone singing?
'I am what I am'
Look out…

19 November 2003

God is God

If you are a Bible reader – maybe a Christian? – you must be sick to the back teeth of all the 'Elvis is God!' rubbish! Nobody, I mean nobody, actually believes that stuff do they?

It all comes from the 1980s I'm a Messiah thing! You could be at a Julian Cope concert and someone says, 'Look, that's God on stage!' Nobody really thinks that Julian Cope is God, apart from Julian Cope, it's all tongue in cheek, isn't it?

Ian McCulloch: everybody knows what I think about his lyrics and the mood of the Bunnymen's music! Yes, I have referred to him as God, but come on! I have stood five yards from him in concert; he's just a man – even a wanker!

Yes, I'm forty-three years old and I shouldn't be saying any of this, but people really do see some celebrities as God! Bollocks! God is God if you're a Christian and believe in all that!!!

20 November 2003

Sour Grapes

Some of my poems…
Could be interpreted as sour grapes?
Hang on!
What would I be famous for?
I'm tone deaf!
And when did you last see a poet on *TOTP*?
I may have a lot to say…
Some strong opinions!
Who cares… no one's listening!
With my illness…
I am famous!
I am 'The Man'
Sour grapes?
I don't think so…

20 November 2003

The Cutter

This Jesus guy (an interpretation)
Was the one I thought would bring it to an end!
Instead it made me realise
I haven't even started the book!
Remember the Bunnymen song 'The Cutter'?
Listen to the words…
That could be the title of my book!
'The Cutter', meaning 'The Truth'!
People top themselves
Because of what's in their head
Even if I found all the right words
And my book was on every coffee table in the land
Nothing would be any different!
It would likely add to the confusion
Fuck you! Mac…
Again it's my illness
That makes this poem…

21 November 2003

Funny Little Man

Here he comes!
It's that funny little man…
Who thinks he's Jesus
Not from heaven, oh no!
It's all very logical!
It's really quite sad…
He has this illness!
He thinks it's a gift…
He's very serious about it all!
Never mind
Who knows?
One day maybe…
When he's dead!

21 November 2003

So Alike

We are all so alike!
More than anyone dare say
This notion of mine…
The whole thing, you must know it by now?
If we are all so alike…
'The wackos', 'The celebrities' even 'Mr Normal'
What makes me different is…
I'm the fool trying to explain everything…
When I find the words
And if it gets published
It will be said…
Big deal, is that it?
My driving force being, all those wackos
That actually believe they're crazy
When we are all so alike!

21 November 2003

So Alike, Part Two

Two-thousand Bunnymen fans at the concert!
Do I really believe I'm the only one getting this message?
The message isn't the problem…
The whole world is getting this message!
Not just from Mac!
It's in nearly everything…
And nearly everyone
Most don't find it a problem!
Most don't even notice…
Take the wackos!
We're not that crazy
We're just told we are
The whole thing can seem like a conspiracy!
We dare not mention a word
It means more medication
Even ECT, fucking hell, come on!
Who are the madmen?

Like, part one…
We're all so alike!

22 November 2003

I'm Your Man

If another human 'Jesus' is OK
I'm your man!
If not?
You're in for a long wait!
Until then…
See ya down the pharmacy

23 November 2003

Before I Die

This is my book of poems!
Entitled *Tomorrow, Today*.
It's you who have to write the new 'Bible'
I would like to see how my birth is written about…
And of course before I die
Because…
When you're dead you're dead!
And I will never have known…

23 November 2003

The Music of Schizophrenia

The television…
Your music collection…
An everyday conversation…
Your mind is constantly recording!
Making memories…
When you have a relapse…
A schizophrenic incident…
Your brain picks out the interesting bits…

On playback…
You can have a right carry on…
Just look at some of my poems!
But hey!!!
That's…
The music of schizophrenia…

26 December 2003

Creation

One of my notions…
We came from 'The Idea'
The idea of 'God Almighty'
A God that had not yet been invented…
'The Bible'
Everything in it!
It's very 'Word'
Only came to be…
When enough people believed in it!
If nobody had read 'The Book'
Well…?
Creation?
Creation came from 'The Idea'
The idea of creation itself
No more, no less…
This poem…
Will only come to be!
If understood by enough…

26 December 2003

Compromise

Like anything…
It really doesn't work!
I've bashed my head from wall to wall…
Maybe I'm too close?
'Wood for the trees'?
Christ! Too late now…

I will be OK…
I'm the joker, a stuntman…
I bend in the wind!
So many don't…
Don't compromise
I did try!

3 December 2003

Standing in Line

Stand up straight!
Speak when spoken to…
Any volunteers?
All step back…
Head in the clouds
Didn't hear the question
Looks like me again?

3 December 2003

Wish Upon a Star

Every question has an answer…
You have to understand 'The Question'
And the answer being given…
Where and whom to ask?
Someone knows who my 'father' is…
For example my father!
If I knew him
To give him the 'Question'
I wouldn't need the 'Answer'
One-day maybe?
Until then!
Keep 'Breathing'!
Keep 'Hoping upon hope'!
If I had a ticket for *Cilla's Christmas Special*
I would shit my knicks!!!!!!!!!!!!!!!!

03 December 2003

This Train

The Glory Train!
Hits town again…
Some suck…
Some work, love and live!
Some are 'Restless'
Need a Buzz!!!
Lock up your 'Daughters'
Hang-on to your 'Sons'
The US may have its 'Twisters'
Over here
It's much more 'Human'…

3 December 2003

All in the Mind

There in my childhood
The doors…
The doors within the mind
As you go through life…
These doors gradually open
The final one being death!
I believe that I have had a quick look…
What I saw was a void of darkness
Really so peaceful…
We all want to explore
And yes it really is…
All in the mind!

28 December 2003

All You Need Is Love

Love, love, love…
Yes, the concept is OK!
The reality quiet different…

We all want the top jobs
But if nobody stacked any boxes
The shops would be empty
Love, love, love…
Fuck! Give me the cash!
I'll find some 'love'
In my own time…

4 December 2003

All We Need Is Love

You see it on TV every day!
Do we really need another 9/11?
Feed the world!
We have so much…
Come on!!!
You could be 'The Man'

4 December 2003

That'll Be the Day

Reminisce watching the film…
I was: The Boy
　　　　The Lover
　　　　The Man…
　　　　The Wand'rin' Star
Forget the past…
Time to move forward!
When I find the 'One'
It really will be the words of the Song!!!
That'll Be the Day
God Bless you, Buddy

4 December 2003

I'm Not Telling the Lie…

Two-and-a-half hours after our 'Xmas Disco'
I find myself back on my PC!
I was kidding myself!
That I was actually saying anything…
They 'Push and Pull'
My Book really was (is) finished!!!
Still you get the same old 'Shit'!
I really hoped, she was the one…
If not… I'm a man, that's OK!
Still they 'Push and Pull'
Christ!!!
'I'm not telling the lie'!!!

5 December 2003

Where?

If you get the chance
If it's not edited
Where did it come from?
OK! It is me…
Jesus Christ! I mean…
You could of so easily have written it!!!
It is partly so innocent…
A bit scary…
Where???

5 December 2003

I'm Not Telling the Lie

Guinea Pigs

Just a boy…
In Denny Crescent
Hours upon hours
With my pet guinea pigs
Building homes
Making runs…
Life was good!
Life was simple…
It was all there…
The birth, the death, the loving the fighting…
You lose so much…
When you grow up!
My little pigs…

5 December 2003

Penultimate

Did I get the girl?
Did I get the farmhouse?
Time my friend…
Time will tell!
Yes, I'm no different from you!
Just a dreamer…
Dare I jest?
A poet who can't spell!!!
Well? Turn the page…
I haven't written it at this moment
But…
What's my last one?

5 December 2003

The Living End

A band from down the Yellow Brick Road…
I have the T-shirt
A couple of years ago at the Astoria
Just their name…
Is inspiration: The Living End
Twenty-first-century rockabilly
Rockabilly punks…
Yes, I know, I'm forty-three, but forty-three years young!!!!!!
Roll on… ROLL ON…

5 December 2003

I.ix

2004

Turn the Key

Freedom is a state of mind…
I myself have always been free!
Sometimes without the grace…
The grace of knowing I was free.
Like most things it has its price
That being…
I'm a prisoner to my very own poetry
Trying to set others free…
Are you free?
Are you ready to turn that key…?

26 January 2004

Do You Think So?

Because I'm so lonely…
So much time on my hands
My imagination can take off…
I actually kid no one
I'm no eighties Messiah!
Not even a very good poet
This Jesus guy…
Do you think so?
…of course not!

2 February 2004

Live on Love

A boy and a girl
Can…
Live on love
A man and a woman
Cannot…
Because a woman
Always wants more
New car
Bigger home
Etc.

11 February 2004

Twenty-three Years

I'm a bit disillusioned
Twenty-three years of your drugs…
Tardive dyskinesia
My tongue just keeps spinning
No one asked me anything
No one said a word
Twenty-three years ago…
You just jumped me!
My joke being 'I'm the second coming'
Well who are you?
Who are you to fill me with your drugs?
Twenty-three years…
In with the shrink last week
He read me some of my recent notes
Still no one listens
Bit of a joke… indeed
Mentally ill?
Someone's opinion
'Status quo'
Whose status quo…?
My tongue just keeps spinning
But hey that's OK!

It's not yours!
Twenty-three years...

22 February 2004

1984, But Take the Pills Anyway!

The other day...
In with the shrink
He read me a line from my notes!
Which was that...
'He believed he was having his photo taken in the town centre'
Which means...
I need medication!
Is he on a different planet?
How many cameras are in the town centre for Christ's sake!
Your words are so easily misinterpreted
You're a joke
You're a mental patient
Next time you're up town...
SMILE!!!

22 February 2004

Going Nowhere...

How many songs do you hear with...
'Going nowhere'?
Everything is rubbish!
Nothing is cool...
Etc, Etc, need I go on?
Even a few of my poems
Go on about boredom, lost dreams etc, etc.
But hey! Hang on a moment...
Blood running through my veins
The wind blowing past your ear lugs
When musicians get their money, usually loads...
They complain about that!
They complain about the system that made them rich!
Get a life!

Nothing is cool… Everything is cool!
Example: the telephone – how cool is that?
Taste buds – how cool?
Life its very self…
How cool is that…?

23 February 2004

Not Even One Day…

What do I want?
What did I want?
This Messiah thing…
It's OK as a dream inside my mind
Lying on my sofa with my music playing
The reality could really suck?
When my family broke up…
I could have done more!
But there it was in my mind
I was destined for bigger things
What do I want?
My farmhouse…
To love and to be loved
Lying on my sofa…
It's all there in my mind
Another ten years
And I'll still be there lying on my sofa
A little sad…
But hey!
Some of those dreams…

23 February 2004

The Dead Don't Walk

If you read in today's newspaper
That someone had walked into a morgue
And had brought someone back to life
After four days
What would you think?

So why do so many believe it…
When they read it in the Bible?
Things that are written…
Make it impossible for you or I to be 'the second coming'
Personally I'm not holding my breath

24 February 2004

Spirit in the Sky

You all know my daughter is a Christian
You've all read some of my poems
Imagine some of the conversations between father and daughter
I don't think she takes much notice
After all, I'm just a funny old man
Occasionally I go along to her church
She's got spirituality big time!
I also have spirituality…
But not from the Bible
The point I try to make is:
The Bible is just a story, a fantasy
My daughter believes every word in black and white
My spirituality comes from my music
But if I'm saying God is a fantasy
How can I claim to have spirituality?
I believe in God as an idea
I don't believe in God as a reality
The spirituality is the same
It's down to definition
It's the need in us all to say there's more…
…is there any more?

25 February 2004

One Million Dollars

Some of the missiles used in war
Cost one million dollars each…
One million dollars!
Take the war in Iraq

Billions of dollars…
Fucking billions!
Imagine those billions being medical supplies, food, etc.
Saddam would have been out in minutes
No conflict, nobody hurt
Yes it's just a poem!
Don't just dream it, DO IT!
One million dollars…

4 March 2004

God Bless America

Two jumbos fly to New York…
Thousands are killed
The world is on fire!
Afghanistan is bombed!
Afghanistan is flattened
Thousands more die…
God bless America
Fuck America!
Thousands more are going to die
What happened to love?
The message from the jumbos
Was: the inequalities in the world.
When Afghanistan was flattened
How many of the dead came back from New York?
None!
9/11 they died for nothing
Give their lives meaning today!
A better world…
Open your eyes!
Look within…
God bless America…

4 March 2004

Dreams of Children

Many would say…
Grow up Colin!

Dreams of children…
Bollocks is my reply!
How many kids command soldiers into battle…?
Plastic soldiers don't bleed!
It's time to change!
Enough is enough
Dreams of children…

4 March 2004

Let's Dance

My daughter,
My son,
We all have had it hard…
I get frustrated with Natalie,
It's only an impression but!
She's so self satisfied
Yes she's had it hard,
Again, we all have had it hard
Nats needs to get her head out of the clouds
Maybe I'm wrong?
My shoes,
Her shoes,
Luke's shoes
Everybody!
Let's dance…

21 March 2004

Love Thy Neighbour

Kick it back
You white honky
Everything far too serious these days
Live a little…
Love a little…
Be true, be honest! At least to yourself
Love thy neighbour
Love your family

Today could be your last?
Kick it back
Kick it up
Love thy neighbour
Sex?
Come on, you know what I'm saying
Love…

21 March 2004

Having a Laugh

HIV
AIDS
Chickenpox
No chance…
God's having a laugh
The joke is you
HIV
AIDS
Chickenpox
Come on…
Dollars in the bank
HIV
AIDS…

23 March 2004

The Dawn of the New Tomorrow, Today

(maybe yesterday?)

We walk in fields
Fields without fences
Meeting new people!
Sharing the fruits of a living planet
No fears, no trouble
Fields without fences
Seeing far-off places
Places we only imagine
Heaven knows this is the time

The time to share!
Believing in yourself
Is just the beginning
Help the blind!
To share the profits of an exciting world
No fears, no trouble
The dawn of the new tomorrow, today
We walk in fields
Fields without fences...

re: 2 April 2004

Jesus Christ

I believe in Jesus Christ the man
I don't believe in Jesus Christ the stories
I believe He was put here to say 'the truth'
Which we all know anyway!
The stories are written by the church
In order to try to keep people in their place
OK, Jesus wasn't a communist
We all need riches for motivation...
One day we may be ready
Ready for 'the truth'
Jesus Christ!
Will we know it when we see it...?

4 April 2004

Blue Suede Shoes

Many years ago...
At our Rockabilly Record Hop!
I would dance and bop...
Around and around making circles
Not unlike...
The Native American
A kitten after its tail...
The stars and planets
Where does it all end?

It ends at its beginning
Maybe death isn't the end?
But a new beginning!
We, the earth, everything
Are all just bits of dust!
Spinning around
Full of electric…
Dancing and bopping
In those blue suede shoes…

7 April 2004

Standing Tall

It's not about you or me
It's not about my book of poems
It's about men standing tall
Brother beside brother
Lying in my bed Easter 2004
Writing yet another poem
One-day maybe?
Men standing tall

9 April 2004

Shot in the Foot

Everybody knows…
Myself!
Friends and family
Staff at 'the Bungalow'
People in the town
The bus driver
I've been shot in the foot!
They can't give me the Lotto
Many would shout: Fix!
It could start a riot
It'd be a laugh
A 'riot'
But seriously…

I'm always going to be skint
Shot in the foot!

21 April 2004

Finally

Everybody telling you…
Nobody listening
You know!
You have always known…
Your music collection
Really is about you…
Again, you've always known!
Watching the TV, fuck!
What can you do?
The world doesn't stop spinning
These poems aren't nothing
Yes, the Lotto would be nice!
Got a tin opener?
Money doesn't come close
Finally…

21 April 2004

Hoops

Life is about 'hoops'
Pulling people through hoops
What happens when you get it?
Are you happy? (Happier?)
Jesus in his day set so many free
They crucified him!
John Lennon the same
They shot the fucker…
The hoop thing will never end…
Who's who anyway?
Ask yourself anything!
Hoops…

30 April 2004

Sleeping Satellite (and a Million Other Songs)

'Sleeping Satellite' by Tasmin Archer
A Number One hit single some years back!
Did every one think they were the 'Sleeping Satellite'?
Maybe they knew one?
If no one had anything better to spend their money on that week?
Why! Give it to me...
Did it even move the units?
Or like so many things, politics, those green doors?
Does 'green' in green door mean jealousy, greener grass, maybe not?
Maybe just those guys who push your button!
Sorry I'm drifting! Back to Tasmin, oh, I'm finished.
Next time you're buying music...
Forget what you've been told!
Rock the boat...

2 May 2004

Get Some Grace

Hey you with your silver spoon
No, not you with your millions
You on the social...
Some would die
And are dying
To be you...
You're led to believe we owe you everything
Maybe, who knows?
But 'get some grace'
Write that book?
Have a beef curry?
For a start, you're in my poem
You know!
Everybody knows...
'Get some grace'

3 May 2004

The Cross of Christ

Walking down the back of Finland Way, my home…
April 2004, a few clouds in the sky
Bright blinding sunshine!
A tear in my eye!
Squinting…
There it was in the sun and the clouds…
The Cross of Christ
Golden…
In your face!
Tell me I'm a liar
Your loss!

3 May 2004

Prisoner

Last night I asked Natalie to the Thunderbird!
For my birthday…
I was going to ask Luke also
Her reply was 'No, but thanks for asking' – no surprise there…
Why, I ask myself?
Because she is promised eternity in 'heaven'
'God'
Or the idea of God
Must be life…
She is walking up this garden path
What's at the end?
We will all find out, that's for sure
Myself?
I'd like to do some living on the way…
Or why did 'God' put breath into my body?
'The Bible'
'The Church'
Takes too many prisoners…

4 May 2004

Fire

Pavitt reads 'We must burn for Christ'
Hey I'm on fire!
Don't tell me about burning!
Pavitt
Has been set free…
I believe he needs setting free again!
I'm told I hang on to things…
Well what's Pavitt doing?
As he bangs his pulpit!
We all know…
Christ! 'Get a life'
Have a cup of tea…
It was the Church that crucified Christ!
It was the Church that put the Bible together…
'Christ the Man' just loved life…
Come on!

4 May 2004

New Guy!

Hey you!
Listen up…
There's a new guy in town!
OK, you shot the sheriff
He had it coming!
But this is the twenty-first century
I'm the deputy
I've had about has much as I'm going to take…
So cut the crap!
Get your act together!
I'm watching…
That's me…
The new guy!

4 May 2004

The Soft Parade

In the video 'The Soft Parade'
Jim says that the Shaman is out for himself…
Maybe?
In my own experience I have to disagree
Yes, I would like some cash!
There's more, oh yes…
When I lose myself
I'm looking for answers
And how to turn those answers into reality
I have always been a dancer
We all hear the music…
It's mostly history now
I was never on my own, lonely yes…
We're all part of the same team
Can you hear them?
Those cavemen…
Some things don't change
And never will…

5 May 2004

Pavitt!

Pavitt!
You're worshiping a man
You fucking hammered to a tree…
No wonder you keep praying!
And you think you're going to heaven
Myself, I'm not praying!
If I was also there?
Christ! I'm not asking for forgiveness
I was just watching!
Why such words I hear you say?
Because I only have words!
You have my daughter…

5 May 2004

X Marks the Spot

Hit that button!
Turn me on…
X marks the spot!
Come to me…
'Dr Love'
I know you inside out!
When we've done
And you're making a cuppa
Your legs will disappear
Turn to jelly…
Hold up!!!
It's just come to me!
This poem could be totally misinterpreted
Fuck! It's just a love song
'I love you'
The rest is up to you…
X marks the spot!
Oh, yes…

14 May 2004

Lost in Music…

Many a moon ago…
This kid went looking for his father
He discovered a path called music
He couldn't believe his ears
It was as if it were meant to be!
The two became one
Johnny Cash, 'A Boy Named Sue' – etc, etc…
It got a bit manic to say the least!
Some girls along the way…
The boy himself could not sing…
His ideas went into poetry
But still!
Lost in music…

15 May 2004

Dark Side of the Wall

The 1980s
Tripping in hospital again
I awoke with a shout!
One of the other wackos
Was into Pink Floyd
Dark Side of the Moon
That night
I was surrounded by *The Wall*
The Pink Floyd movie
My own hand came up!
With the final brick…
The breath went from my body!
I awoke with a scream
Dark side of the wall…

19 May 2004

Jesus Christ is a Teddy Boy…

Out of date…
Out of fashion…
Nobody wants him!
Nobody needs him!
But, oh! Those heads that turn!
…as you walk through the town
Out of date…
Out of fashion…
Nobody wants him!
Nobody needs him!
Christ is a Ted…
Rock 'n' roll… lives!

2 June 2004

They, Could Be You…

They build you up…
They knock you down
Time and time again!
Where is it all going?
They build you up!
Leave you for a while…
Then, as usually…
Send in the bulldozers
Up down
Back to front, sideways
Who's pushing whom?
They build you up…
They knock you down!
But who?
The who, could be you, yourself…

2 June 2004

Waves Come and Gone

TOTP tonight, nothing!
Absolutely nothing…
Six months riding the wave
'Fantastic!'
Medication?
Take it or leave it…
Same music collection!
Not that important…
Until the next time…
Waves!

4 June 2004

Just What I Don't Need!

Constantly on the TV
Constantly in the music!

Give it a rest, please!
Sex, sex, sex,
New romantic?
Old romantic…
I'm sticking to my guns
Holding out for love…
Sex?
Get a life!
I hear you say…
Bollocks!

6 June 2004

Only Bad News is News!

For example:
Ice cream man drives up
Gives all the kids a free ice cream
No big deal…
The same ice cream man
Takes a gun
Shoots a couple of the kids…
Frontpage news
News at Ten
Etc, etc…
What I'm really trying to say is…
'Mental health' gets bad press!
One madman out of hundreds
It's him who makes the news
What happened to all the free ice creams?

7 June 2004

Last Breath

A writer like myself…
Isn't finished until the end!
His last breath!
Maybe?
The real 'second coming'

Will step out of the clouds…
I hope to watch my kids go through life…
Not much of a hand in their childhood
Sad but true!
Talking of families
Will I ever meet my father?
Secretly…
I like to believe he's in my life
A real live guardian angel
But hey that's another story…
Until then!
My last breath

7 June 2004

I.x

Top of the World, 2004

The Rainbow

Where am I?
What am I doing?
And why?
I've come to the end of my book…
My story of poems
I wasn't prepared for this!
This being nothing…
No pot of gold!
No happy ever after…
Yes it's all a fairytale!
A dream…
Maybe the Lotto?
But how long? And maybe never
The end of my rainbow
A fairytale…
A fairytale that never believed in me…
I'm still breathing
Still dreaming…
The Rainbow…

12 August 2004

Selling the Dream

You read a book
You go to the movies
Buy some music…
Usually you're touched by the story…
Lifted by the film
Maybe dance your socks off!

The Rainbow

The mistake I so often make…
Is that I can live the dream in the story
To a degree I do live the dream
But the dream doesn't put food on the table!
God bless the DWP!
Wake up!!!
You have to have your own…
Chronicles of Narnia
And of course even then…
You have to try and get it into the machine
Selling your dream!

12 August 2004

It Cost Too Much

Put it out…
It cost too much
Too much!
Try once, twice
Don't give yourself a hard time
When you're ready
It will just happen
Myself?
I tried for years!
Then one day, no more
I often think about one…
Still after all this time
But no!
It cost too much
Too much

12 August 2004

Top of the World

Back in the mid 1970s
There was this play on the TV
Even after all this time
It's still in my mind!

There was this guy…
Who filled in the pools coupon
In such a way
They knew he was the one!
They put him in this room
An apartment at the top of the world
He was alone…
By himself!
I was a young teenager
I was inspired
I always wondered
What the numbers might have been?
I now know the combination
Look at me, alone…
By myself!

15 August 2004

Daydream Believer

Sadly this is one of the reasons…
I'm on my own
Head in the clouds!
Dreams don't feed the baby
It's not just writing the song
It's being part of the machine
Right place, right time, right people
Until then…
Daydream believer!

18 August 2004

Schizophrenic by Design

The other day, I asked my mother…
'Were you on any drugs when I was a baby?'
It wasn't a good time!
She got a bit angry
But 'No' was the reply!
I then said, 'What about my father?'

She walked out the room!
He was an airman in the RAF
It could have been part of the plan…
Schizophrenic children!
Tell me I'm wrong!
But these poems of mine
Didn't come from nowhere…
'Schizophrenic by design'
Along with thousands of others!

23 August 2004

All Change

If and when my book gets published…
And if and when it takes off!
All change!
All change? I hear you say
Yes!
The mentally ill, all become well…
And poor old Mr Normal goes crazy
The book tells the ill
What they have always known
But Mr Normal?
Well…
All change!

29 August 2004

Snowballs

Some of my poems…
Kinda follow on from one another
If I'm writing a lot…
And on a similar subject
They can and do snowball
If Jesus in his day
Did actually say all that stuff
He himself may very well have been snowballing
Trying to please…

So many subjects and things
Can and do snowball!
Hey! Slow down
Where are we all going?
Myself?
I'm going to build a snowman!
With snowballs…

29 August 2004

The Second Coming

No! I am not the second coming
But I am likely the nearest you're going to get
I won't be heard about for at least…
Another hundred years or so
That's so the church can make up their stories
Something like…
'And He walked across Corby boating lake'
Get the picture?
So OK I'm not Jesus
But look at some of my poems…
Don't crucify me!
And yes OK
I'll be your Man!
That's in another hundred years or so
OK?

1 September 2004

Different

I have been here…
In the mental health system
Twenty-four years!
I always believed that I was special
Different from the others!
This year it hit me!
It's not that I'm not special
It's that we are all special…

Another thing!
Everybody's the same
We are not second-class
I sometimes looked at the others
Thinking 'What do they know?'
Don't kid yourself!
Yes I am different
We are different
But no different from you!

2 September 2004

Green Day Idiot

Green Day on MTV 2
Complaining about US politics
The millions Bush is making.
How many millions
Are Green Day set to make?
And their corporate record company
Green Day idiot
And bureaucracy!
I'm out of here…
Where?
Down the local record shop
For my very own
American idiot!

22 September 2004

Rat Race

Slow down…
Where do you think you're going?
Get out the race
Food on the table
Roof overhead!
So many racing around…
Like the wheel in a hamster cage

Chill out!
Cup of tea
Pill on tongue
Rats…
Who needs 'em?

22 September 2004

The Vision

Forget the 'Jesus' thing
Many have seen
Some share
'The Vision'
I was there…
I helped shape it
Many have made money
Some never will
When I try to bring it up…
The subject is quickly changed
I walk alone…
Many walk alone
'The Vision'
No not 'Jesus'
But yes, that kinda thing
'The Vision'

8 October 2004

They Didn't Tell Me

They showed me sex
They showed me death
They showed me birth
Love?
The little bastards
They didn't tell me!

11 October 2004

Fox Hunting

It's the people in the towns…
It's the Nanny State
Get a grip!
Unfortunately some things are cruel
Government!
So it's OK to ban it?
One little fox
What about our boys?
Our boys at war!
Come on it's the twenty-first century
Sort it out!
…forget the fox

18 October 2004

Rockabilly Rebel

Why do so many abuse drugs?
Why?
Alcohol the same!
Is it… life is dull?
Is it… the rebel in us?
Kill the stigma…
Kill the rebel, maybe?
From what I can make out…
I need medication
Because without it
I end up like those who abuse it
Me? High on life!
Life is a trip…
I always did do things differently
Hey! That's me…
Rockabilly Rebel

18 October 2004

Problem

If you are reading this
It probably means I have found a publisher.
If you yourself have a problem
Write your own poem about it…
Never say never!
If you are reading this
Thanks!
Twenty-five years…
And I ain't stopping now!

18 October 2004

I Saw the Light

Late 1979
Early 1980
I saw the light
It's took me twenty-four years
To get this far…
Many pills
A few hospitals
To my dying day
I'll never get it all down
Wow!
I saw the light…

22 October 2004

Judgement Day

When I stand before Christ…
I will pay for my sins
Do my time…
That's my ticket!
I didn't crucify anyone!

Christ! Never died for me…
What's your ticket?

6 November 2004

I'm Fucked

Back in '79
I was doing this cartoon strip in an R 'n' R fanzine
It was then I 'saw the light'
And my life went to pieces…
To this day
Pop stars are singing to me
Fiction films about me…
Bollocks to you all!
It's all rubbish…
Back off!!!
Keep your stories
Shove your pop songs
There is nothing I can do
Nowhere I can go
It's in your face!
I'm fucked!

7 November 2004

The Millionaire

I am a millionaire
I have no cash, yet!
Spiritually I'm loaded…
You may not know me personally
But I'm in you all…
The dreamer
The lover
The millionaire…

7 November 2004

Something's Missing

Cash?
The farmhouse?
A big car?
If I got lucky…
I would still be the same
Something's missing!
My father…

7 November 2004

Dear Luke

Don't go looking for things
That ain't there…
Twenty-five years writing this book
And I don't really know any more…
Than when I started.
Life is a gift!
Be happy…
No regrets!
Love Dad xxx

14 November 2004

Psychobilly Cadillac

Have you heard the song
'One Piece at a Time'
By Johnny Cash?
If not, look it up…
Because this book is my
'Psychobilly Cadillac'
Johnny Cash

Sadly…
Another in R 'n' R heaven

19 November 2004

Just Sex!

When pop stars sing…
Usually it's about sex or love
The mistake I always make…
Is that they are singing to me personally
And that it's not about sex…
But the love of mankind
When the reality is
It's just sex!
When will I learn?
Just sex!

21 November 2004

All of Us…

The Bible is a clever book!
It can explain a lot…
But no more than you can teach yourself.
The second coming is a joke!
It's in the English language itself
It's about sex…
When I have my 'bipolar' relapses
My mind is open!
And I can see everything.
Jesus is the TV.
A shotgun in *EastEnders*
Surely is telling you not to get one!
Some use the Bible
To have control over others.
The Bible isn't about Jesus…
It's about the man they want him to be.
Jesus knew this;

Look within –
It's in all of us…

21 November 2004

ABC

Ya go to school!
Ya go to college?
Ya go to university?
Some know so much!
So intelligent
They can't see…
The wood for the trees
One plus one
ABC
1, 2, 3
That's it!
There is no more…
Birds and bees…
Where's the key?

25 November 2004

Why the Tease?

We all know!
The cat is out the bag…
It's me you're looking for!
I'm not messing about…
That's you!
Trying to sell a few more discs
Yes, it's frustrating
If you have any plans?
Come on!
If not?
Why the tease?
Birds and bees…

26 November 2004

Shout to the Top

The Style Council
Blasting out my radio!
1984…
All these years later…
It hits me!
It's me, the one at the top!
The one everyone's wishing for…
Wish Upon a Star
Head in my hands…
Screaming!
It's always been me…
Dim star?
Bright star?
Give me the time…
Shout, wish?
It ain't over yet!

28 November 2004

I'm Ready!

I have the words…
I have my book!
My time is close…
Tomorrow maybe?
Is it people?
Is it God above?
Whatever!
Whenever!
I'm ready…

28 November 2004

Christmas 2004

Peace on earth?
Christmas 2004

Never say never!
We have the technology
Come on…
Bush
Bin Laden
Anyone?
Peace on earth!
Christmas…
Always…

28 November 2004

Bono

I've been listening to Bono and his band…
Bono with his millions of fans
Can't seem to bring world peace.
Take me, lying in my bed…
Scribbling some old poems
Do I really think anyone's listening?
Schizophrenics have a common delusion
Which is, that the world spins around them
Read my poems, if only, hey?
Back to Bono!
Bono sings to me personally!
Listen to his words…
I like to tell myself…
He reads my poems
Hey I'm schizophrenic, anything's possible!
Bono
Ian McCulloch
Myself…
In my world…
We're all friends
One day maybe?

28 November 2004

Bono #2

To correct the last poem!
Bono ain't on *News at Ten…*
Singing 'Sunday Bloody Sunday'
But millions have seen and know of the song!
Music does make a difference!
Achtung Baby
All That You Can't Leave Behind
Vertigo
Can, and do, bring a tear to my eye…
Depending on my mood
'Bono, mine's a lager'
'Mac?'
Well, Bono's got the money…

28 November 2004

The End

This is my last poem!
The End
Damn another one…
OK! Just one more,
It's a bit like life…
The end doesn't have an end
Life goes on and on…

29 November 2004

Are You the One?

I hold the flame…
Deep in the pit of my stomach
It's really the most!
Flickering in its beauty

Are you ready?
Are you the one?

29 November 2004

Enough is Enough

Wednesday first of December 2004
Enough is enough!
Twenty-two years of Bungalow drop-ins
Why?
Come on!
Enough is enough…

1 December 2004

Lights Out!

We all have seen the light!
But what do you do…
When the off switch is broken?
Medication to help you sleep?
Pills and shit…
ECT?
The light of life…
Is really so fantastic!
But when it's all you know…
Fuck!
God, anyone?
Turn out the lights!

1 December 2004

Outside Looking In

Outside looking in
The party's going with a swing
Whose party is it?
Maybe they'll let me in?

Outside looking in
There he is!
But that's me?
Performing and entertaining
Whose party?
My party!
Outside looking in

2 December 2004

Start Again

Give me the 'Electric'
Fry me brains
Spring clean my head…
Start again!

2 December 2004

II.i

Moving On… 2005

Haunted Houses

Three minutes and counting…
The man on the radio spouting
Poems that listeners have sent in!
Airing their works and flouting
And Big Ben said ten!
For women and for men…
Busy workers rushing to their offices
To watch the clocks again!
No time for poetry or poets
For vandalism ruled the day!
Drugs and glue sniffing ruled over the world
If only they would stop, think and say
666 psychos are on the way!
We cooked them lunch the other day
Hungry people in queues!
Lunchtime is here, we all pay our dues…
Nothing is new scoobydoo!
Scrappy left out 'oh boo hoo hoo'
Haunted houses here we come!
No more counting minutes, we are safe now, and home

22 January 2005

Don't Look Back in Anger?

I've been looking back again…
Asking myself different questions
I believe it's all there, in your childhood
Why? And who am I…?
Well? I found something new…
Which hurts so much, I might be getting somewhere?

Mick Mason
He wasn't my father!
But he was my first Dad
A boy needs a 'man'
Someone to look up to…
It was summer '67 maybe '68?
My heart was broken
My brain didn't work any more…
I don't think anybody took much notice?
Years later, when I was a sea cadet
I'm sure I saw him in Plymouth as a sailor
When I knew him, he was in the RAF
It's them…
Messing with my mind
Don't look back in anger?
Who the fuck are Oasis!

23 January 2005

Shout!

Shout! Shout!
Keep it out…
Shout! Shout!
Shout out loud…
The walls keep it in
Who would help?
If they heard you shout
Keep it out!
The law is…
Shout! Shout!
The law is!
Take it, and shout!
If they heard you shout
Who could help?
Shout! Shout!
Keep it out…
Shout! Shout!
Shout out loud…

28 January 1991

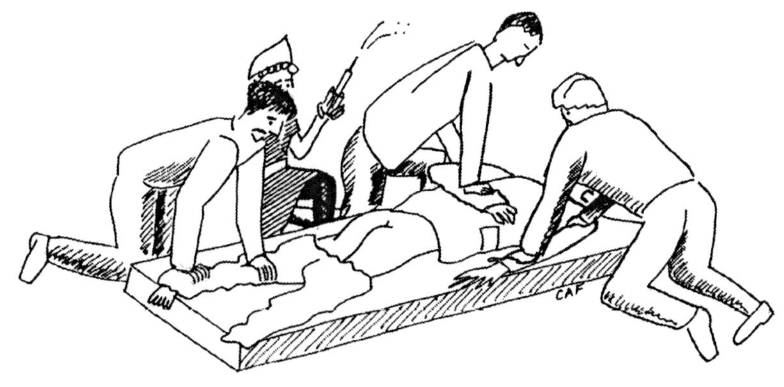

Shout!

The Internet

The Internet is like sex!
If you haven't got it
You may think you're missing out…
But if you have got it?
No big deal…

23 January 2005

My Illness

'My illness'
Isn't just something which happened –
In my childhood or otherwise…
It is chemical
When it happens
I can feel myself change
'The illness'
Or at least the symptoms
Can and do inspire many Hollywood stories
Or does the illness
Nick the ideas from Hollywood?

Chicken or the egg?
'My illness'
Good or bad?
It's my lot in life!
I'm me!
You are you!
Get on with it…

24 January 2005

Possibilities

I'm what you would call a natural
Never abused drugs…
High on life
The possibilities of life
Concoct some plans
And just take off!
The possibilities
Music…
Love?
Come?
Fly with me…

24 January 2005

No Prisoners!

If at any time these poems of mine become something
i.e. that 'second coming' rubbish
My book of words…
Should not be used to take prisoners!
i.e. like the church has got my daughter
OK! Governments need to defend the land
But why have we enemies in the first place?
Will 'Man' never learn?
We all know, Good and Bad!
Come on…
No prisoners!

24 January 2005

Enlightenment

'Enlightenment'
Is not what it's cracked up to be!
When you get it...
What do you do?
Stare into space...
We all get there one day!
Does it ease off?
Hey!
It cracks me up...

25 January 2005

Heaven?

I believe you can only go to heaven if you believe in heaven – because it's believing in heaven that makes heaven.
When Jesus talked about heaven, he was inventing it with all its many mansions, but he couldn't build those mansions without all of us, because it's the idea of heaven that makes heaven.
This poem doesn't knock heaven! I want people to believe, because it's the believers who make it, and yes I'm becoming a believer.
But my way! And of course not without the man Jesus
When or if people stop believing, it will just disappear...
Heaven is in the idea...

25 January 2005

Heaven

God?

'God' is also an idea
In the idea,
You might not believe in God…
What have you then?
OK! You may not go to church…
You may not own a Bible
But…
Look within!
If you don't know?
Who…
'The idea'

25 January 2005

Running Free…

My grandparents are free
Running free…
Laid to rest
In Langford graveyard
Forever summer
Across Langford common
Cartwheeling
Running free…
In the breeze
I believe…

26 January 2005

Members Only

Reality can be…
And so very often is
Looking at a brick wall
But have they looked within?
Hey! The Party

It's priceless…
Someone's reality?
May not be your reality
And vice versa
Your head?
Members only!
It's priceless…

26 January 2005

Simple

Life?
Life is so simple!
The sun shines
The earth spins
Communication…
That's the problem!
Life?
So simple…

28 January 2005

Moving On…

It says in the Bible somewhere…
Christ the second coming!
Will rule for 'one thousand' years
So OK!
It's the words in my book
That will rule…
In which case!
Somewhere around the Third Millennium
Look out!
Watch and wait…
A new set of words
A new book!
I'm not trying to change the Bible
I'm moving it on…
Just as it will move on!
A thousand years from now…

28 January 2005

The Devil?

All these songs…
About the 'Devil'
'The Devil made me do it!'
Bollocks!
The Devil is history…
He never made you do a thing!
This is the twenty-first century
It's about the individual!
You yourself…
Forget the Devil!
That's bullshit…
Maybe Hollywood?
It's you!
The individual
And always was…

28 January 2005

Destiny…

Bono
Mac
Myself
Having a pint!

29 January 2005

What About the Girl?

It's my destiny…
To write these words
Another destiny!
'Gold' oh yes
The words…
The book!
Has its own destiny
With or without me…
That's three destinies
One down

Two to go!
What about the girl?

29 January 2005

Until Then…

Money?
The root of all evil
One day?
But not today
We may be ready
To live without
The next book?
The Third Millennium
But for now
'Gold'
Give us the Gold!
Until…

30 January 2005

No More Excuses…

Jesus!
The Third Millennium
If we haven't got it right then…
Why did we bother?
The Third Word
Will be everything!
No more excuses!
If not?
Press the Button…
Over and out!

30 January 2005

Back to the Bungalow

Back to the Bungalow
Cup of tea…
Old friends
New friends
'The Devil you know'
But do I?

30 January 2005

May 2005

May 2005?
Forty-five years old…
The 'Gold'
But if still no Gold?
1-2 5-6 9-11
Lucky dip
Shove it
Shove the lot!
The farm, everything…
Up your ass!

20 February 2005

Denial

'Bipolar'
'Schizophrenia'
Labels…
Just labels!
Being in denial
I'm saying I know what I'm in denial of…
I know myself…
110 per cent
Do you?

22 February 2005

Zodiac Mindwarp

Zodiac Mindwarp
Kill or cure!
Kill or cure!
Sexual hang-ups?
Zodiac Mindwarp
Turn up the volume…
Mindwarp…
Kill or cure!
Kill or cure!
Sexual hang-ups?
Kill or cure…

11 February 1991

In the Clouds

I once heard it said…
'You can never fly high enough'
Two years…
Not bad for a nobody!
If you don't mind
I'll step down awhile
Catch my breath…
Walk in my shoes?
No! Fly…

28 February 2005

I'm Not a Killer!

If you believe…
Jesus personally died for you
Your sins, whatever
That must mean…
You, yourself personally killed him
Get it?
For my trip to heaven…
I never killed anyone
Translate the Bible all you like…
I'm not a killer!

1 March 2005

Zodiac Mindwarp

Shepherd and the Sheep

It's a joke!
It's a laugh…
Walking through town
Some look, heads turn…
Me? I'm deceiving no one
Never led anybody astray
They led themselves
Fooled themselves
'Shepherd and the sheep'
Who's laughing?
Me? No not me,
But…

3 March 2005

The Other Side

When you break through!
Step through?
Or just find yourself
The other side…
Are you clever?
Lucky, unlucky?
Never mind, we all get there…
It's in front of you all the time!
It can be taboo
Does it have a name?
Born again?
Born-again Christian?
Or just part of growing up…
If you know what I'm saying?
You may have a smile
If you are puzzled?
I'm just trying to help…
But don't be a smart ass!
The other side…

3 March 2005

Shepherd and the Sheep (Part Two)

If everybody were reading my poems...
Yes, I could well be 'The Shepherd'
But...
The Shepherd and the Sheep
Ain't what I'm about...
I may shine a light...
For some of us in darkness
But, in my words...
We are all spiritually the same
And share the same Enlightenment.
If that makes me a leader
So be it...
But who's reading my words?
Or at least, in my life time...?

3 March 2005

Captain Scarlet

Looking in the rearview again
Childhood heroes...
Captain Scarlet
Dig up the road!
Smash down some old buildings
The Mysterons are still here!
So OK –
If I'm Scarlet
Who's pulling my strings?
Childhood heroes...
Scarlet!
He's ya Man...

3 March 2005

Pretty Little Angel Eyes

How many times have you heard?
'God is looking down from above'
Think about that a moment

From above?
Where above?
It makes more sense...
That if we are all a part of 'God'
God would be looking out through our eyes
Yours and mine...

3 March 2005

In Dreams

Night time...
When you close your eyes
What do you see?
Where do you go?
I myself, become part of it all
The universe
I close my eyes
The darkness is blinding
The void
Which is my mind
Becomes everything...
Only at night
We are free...
Above the trees
You and me...

3 March 2005

Steve Barratt 1960–2000

Steve, Kathy, Tony and myself were some psycho Rockabilly Rebels, gigs here, gigs there, myself at the wheel.

OK, let's go! Have you seen the film *Big Fish*? Because Steve was a storyteller, not fancy or fantasy, basically just lies. I always asked myself, why? When I saw the film *Big Fish* I had a tear in my eye: that was Steve! Steve the star! I don't ask why any more.

Before I knew Steve, I would see him standing in the Thunderbird with a different coloured quiff every time! Blue, orange, red, etc. My friend Gary first spoke with him; our friendship came about when I was with Maggie a little later.

Steve and myself were both record collectors! Psychobilly. We had this rivalry – it was part of the friendship, we often disagreed over nothing! Again that was our friendship!

Steve also had this habit of talking with people the other side of the hall, with both of them looking over, as if it were me they were talking about. This was maybe paranoia but it always happened!

Near the end... Steve married Penny... He had this disease, 'Crohns'. Tony and myself have talked since and we believe he knew he didn't have long to live, but gigged and rocked 'n' rolled till the end; that's one story he didn't tell us!

The day I went to pay my respects, as he laid in his coffin I played one of our rockabilly songs in my car: 'Ice Cold' by Restless; he would have liked that!

Steve was not a 'Christian', even more he was a 'Psychobilly', but in my philosophy he knew the score! Yes! In my heart he is in heaven, maybe telling or even living some of those old stories he once told...

7 March 2005

Magic on the Number Three

Here she comes!
The number three
'Disabled facilities'
All mod cons
Ticket to the town
All day that is...
Now I've my car
I miss the star!
People talking...
This 'n' that
Some you know...
Magic!
That's what it was
She's a star!
Corby Star...

8 March 2005

Magic on the Number Three

My Moment?

Some may say…
I've had my moment!
And blew it…
I disagree
I saw it coming…
And had a ball
You are not me!
You don't know my philosophy…
TV? I was all over the place
What now?
Waiting for the cheque?
Maybe, maybe not…
My moment?
My party?
I'll be back…

8 March 2005

The Master Plan

We all watch TV
We all love Hollywood
Stories…
Fact or fiction, we love 'em
We all like to believe…
We're part of a bigger picture
The Master Plan!
So OK, ask yourself…
What's that one then?
No, not Oasis
It's the Bible, oh yes,
How many bother with that?
OK then…
Write your own words
Be the Master
In your own Master Plan…
Come on!
Rock 'n' roll…

8 March 2005

Change of Heart…

Book One!
Twenty-five years to write
Mostly
Nearly all the way
I said…
When you're dead you're dead!
Book Two?
Just started it
A change of heart
Trying to work it out
Heaven?
There has to be something…
Why?
The meaning of life…
Why?
Heaven…
One we will all know…
Walking up the garden path
Or not?
As the case may be…

8 March 2005

Come on Mac…

I lay upon my sofa…
Music spinning around!
Lonely!
But not alone…
My friends sing to me…
Write songs for me!
New Bunnymen album soon
Come on Mac…
Lonely
But not alone…

9 March 2005

Hang on to a Dream

The farmhouse…
The girl…
Hang on to the dream?
How long?
No I'm not bitter
A little sad…
The farm?
The girl…

9 March 2005

End of Part One, Book Two

One chapter closes
Another one opens
When my books are finished
You can nip to see the end
But for now?
End of part one, book two

9 March 2005

II.ii

Come Together 2005

Come Together

Churches…
Up and down the land
Across the world
Communist
Buddhist
Everybody…
Stop disagreeing
Calling it something different
Just to be different
Forget the ten o'clock rubbish
All the bad stuff
Come together…
I'm human
You're human
Just human…

9 March 2005

You and Me…

Famine
War
Killing
Good and bad?
In the ideal world…
Peace and love
Maybe not…
Maybe we need some bad
Do we?

60/40?
80/20?
It's not down to you
Or me
Famine?
War?
If not you and me
Who?

9 March 2005

Prince Charming

Going to waste…
All this wit and charm
Alone night after night
Even Cinderella
Had two sisters…
And some mice
But if I do have all this charm
Why am I…
By myself
Prince Charming?
What's the point…
On your own?

12 March 2005

This Girl…

This girl…
She knows whom
She knows what I'm saying
Body language
Chemistry
It's all there…
I say to her…
When I've my millions
She knows…
The ball is in her court
If? The above

Why wait?
Do I need the millions?
Body language
Chemistry
Love!
It isn't always enough
This girl…
She knows whom

12 March 2005

I Feel Like Crying

Just back from Mum's
Sunday dinner…
Thirteenth March
Holding back the tears
Closest I've seen it in a long time
Mum and Dad splitting
No big fight, no…
Sad and bitter, maybe?
What do we all have?
Dad, working and watching the telly
Mum? I'm not sure
A bit of a dream world like myself, maybe?
Again what do we have?
Any of us…
I feel like crying…

13 March 2005

Running

Running…
Keep on running
Running to the future
One eye in the rearview
Running!
Always running…

13 March 2005

Black and White

These poems of mine…
Are not me 'black and white'
Some bits are poetic licence
Making bits fit!
Never had a hit single
Can't even sing!
The 'New Bible' line…
Never got me laid!
Many more I think?
But you get the picture
Wait a moment!
Most of it is me…
Loads left out
And some to come…

13 March 2005

Movie Star

Ever thought of being a star?
The hero!
In your very own blockbuster
Well take a look at yourself
That's what you are
The hero!
The movie star!
Playing yourself
In your very own lead roll
Real life…
Movie star!
We all are…

14 March 2005

Wacko Jacko

If you are a down and out
Prison…
Is a step up
But for wacko jacko
Prison…
Is a long way down
Anyhow
Where were the parents
At that time…?

15 March 2005

Runaway…

Exhausted and tired
Missing deadlines
Somewhere up north
Motorway cafe
Belinda Carlisle
'Runaway Horses'
Listening to the words!
Van parked outside…
Why?
Why am I working?

15 March 2005

Heaven!

Still with…
Belinda
Heaven on earth?
Not two miles away
Just over the hill
Great Oakley!
The farm…

Heaven…
Oh yes!

15 March 2005

The Car!

Recently I've heard this question…
Many times, on the radio and TV
'What car would Jesus drive?'
That's an easy one…
Put yourself in his shoes
Volvo 850
Easy!
Obvious…

15 March 2005

Cake?

Give me my cake
I wanna stuff myself…
Make myself sick!
Don't want your fame
Just the cake!
You can have the words…
Give me the cake!
I wanna be sick!
Sick everywhere…
Get it?

15 March 2005

From Within

What's the point?
Being a rebel…
And spending your life in jail
Take your time…

Work it out?
Then set the world on Fire!
Rockabilly Rebel?
No!
Psychobilly
From within
Within the system!

15 March 2005

Feet on the Ground!

Standing at the foot of the mountain
Didn't fall, no...
Lonely at the top...
In the clouds
Just as it's painful
Alone, in the crowd...
At least up the mountain...
You're nearer your dreams
Real or not real...

15 March 2005

Calm Down

Calm down!
Have a cigarette?
That only calms you down
If you are addicted
A nicotine addict!
So if not?
Deep breaths...

15 March 2005

Skeletons

Writing this book...
It's everything!

Everything about myself…
'Skeletons under the stairs'
Skeletons?
Sorry I do have a couple!
So ashamed!
Also a criminal…
But if I'm Truman
In the *Truman Show*?
Then you all already know…
If you missed that one?
One day maybe…
Or not!

15 March 2005

Skeletons (Part 2)

Looking back…
So obvious!
Obviously a set-up
Does that make it any different?
Set-up or not…
I still did it!
Medication
Can make you a yes man
When you mean no…
Trying to please!
That's medication…
Another one?
Working for the council!
Left alone…
So obvious!
A set-up…
But again, I still did it
I cannot forgive myself
Especially that one!
Set-up or not…
I still did it…

16 March 2005

Dawn, Today

Listen to the birds
They are singing…
Singing for you and me
Rushing about for work?
Kids to school?
Slow down…
The day will still happen
Look around yourself…
Catch your breath
Listen to the birds
Singing!
Dawn, today…

16 March 2005

Guinea Pigs?

I once heard it said…
Guinea pigs?
What's the point of a guinea pig?
Well?
What's the point of humans?
Anything?
Living and breathing!
Life!
At least guinea pigs…
Don't kill one another!

16 March 2005

Naked

Sitting on the other side!
Naked…
You feel naked
Your mind open

You see and understand everything
Vulnerable?
Your life is open…
Back to normality?
Dressed…
Watch out!
A streaker…

16 March 2005

Heaven? #3

We have looked at…
Heaven the idea!
Also, heaven on earth
A very personal view
What have we now?
Six numbers on a Saturday night?
Or maybe, sex?
We all know the six numbers!
Sex? Well…
Back in the 1950s
Up until the late 1970s
This was referred to as heaven
That is of course in music
Well that could mean the Creation
Conception!
If we end up in heaven
Maybe we come from heaven?
Personally…
I'm with, it's in the idea

18 March 2005

Heaven? #4

Back to…
Heaven on earth?
That could be England
The West? The USA

But how many are miserable?
That can't be it!
Africa?
The Third World…
Some sing all day
Just being happy in yourself
Is a start!
Heaven?
We'll all know!
Soon enough…

18 March 2005

Levi Dexter

Tonight! Saturday 19 March 2005, Levi's first UK gig in 20 years and I'm going to be there! Ace Cafe, north London! Below is a write-up I did for the CD release of *Levi Dexter & the Ripchords – Tear it Up Live 1981*. RAUCD 159 Raucous Records 2004. Also one of my drawings is on the disc, also see below, cheers Danny and Howard!

19 March 2005

Levi Dexter and the Ripchords 1980–1981, a collaboration of US roots rockers and the passion of UK rockers! To my regret I only caught them the once, Dingwalls sometime in '81. Some might say these cats and others killed rock and roll, I have to disagree! The 1970s were over, a new decade needed new blood: 'Rockabilly Punks'. Punks, I hear you say? Well, what was Elvis if not the original Punk?!!! I remember pickin' up the *…In The Beginning* EP, Caister that year; I was telling this girl, 'Listen, listen, IT'S THE BEAT.' I was young, a new generation, and Levi said it all!!! What happened? Why? Record deals… Big business? Who knows…? Recently on briansetzer.com *Stray Cats at the Hoot* a photo of Levi and Danny B entitled 'Rockabilly Royalty' – need I say more?

Spring 2004

Levi Dexter

Too Safe!

Last night!
Levi Dexter
North London…
Rock 'n' roll is too safe?
Levi rocked
Oh yes!
The crowd stood
Stood and watched
And clapped
This is the Ace Cafe London
Come on…
Rock 'n' roll
I was asked to calm it
Christ?
I'm not dead!
Too safe…
New blood?
I don't think so…

20 March 2005

Buskin'

The year? Probably 1988, up-town Corby town! I had just learnt one chord from Ashley, a friend of mine, I remember! I didn't really use that chord, I just thrashed at the guitar, but I did get a rhythm, just with no proper musical notes. But again, a good rhythm!

The songs? 'Silver' by the Bunnymen! It has this great line: 'Man has to be his own saviour'. That line inspired me to fight my illness. I slipped in a couple of my poems and a whole bunch of one-lines from different songs! For example, 'Get Me to the World on Time' by the Electric Prunes, and the song 'Pushin' Too Hard' by Sky Saxon and the Seeds.

The girls? I was not tuneful, but I was loud! Heads would keep popping in and out of the shops! It was the girl shop assistants eyeing me up! There was one guy, he gave me a pound! It was when I was doing

'Silver', maybe for the second time!

Trouble? There was this gang of young men, spinning pennies at me! Not at my feet no, there were trying to hit my head or face! I just carried on, God knows why. I was probably having too much fun!

Buskin'? I only did it the once in Corby – maybe the spinning pennies put me off. A couple of times in Kettering and once in Northampton! Great fun! I put a lot of enthusiasm into it but with cool!

1993! My big moment… I was asked if I would like to do a spot on stage in front of about 150 ex-punk rockers! Fantastic! Lights, PA, everything! I myself made a recording of it, which I sometimes try to sell a cassette of! It took place at the Corn Market Hall, Kettering. Ian McCulloch, my number one man, was in the middle of his solo stuff, and Steve Humphreys, Mac's drummer, was at the gig! Double fantastic! Steve knew I was a fan of Mac and we talked a little…

Bottle? No, I have not lost the bottle, I suppose I just need a reason. No! I just need somebody to ask! I'm ya Man!

20 March 2005

Let It Go…

We all get high…
We all get the lows…
It's the fool
That won't let it go…
Refuelling in flight?
What happens?
When spaceships crash
Let it go…

20 March 2005

In the Name of God…

President Bush
And the American people…
Make me nervous!
Trigger-happy America
Bush himself wouldn't blow the world up
But Bush 'In the name of God' would

Maybe propaganda?
I don't think like this by accident…

20 March 2005

That's Life!

When things happen…
My daughter would say
That's God!
I say…
No Natalie
That's life
Many things in my life
I would say…
That's a set-up!
Hang on!
Maybe not…
Maybe that's life also
God?
Coincidence?
Set-up?
That's life!

21 March 2005

Dig 'Em Up?

Out in my motor!
The mods…
Scooter boys!
I always smile
I always say…
'Dig 'em up'
Time too!
Dig up some Rockabillies
Come on!
Rock 'n' roll

21 March 2005

Evolution

My life…
'Schizophrenia'
Whatever?
I like to believe
It's part of evolution
I toy with the idea
These feelings…
Mean something
When really it's nonsense
Cavemen had these feelings
Sexual desire
Sexual gratification
Motivation
I'm just a caveman
Trying to please…
Do you like my painting?

21 March 2005

Tsunami?

Sucking the milk
From the Mother
Oilfields dry up
The rainforest
Chopped and gone
The air is thin
Thunder and lightning
Earthquakes
Tidal waves
Tsunami?
A warning
End days…

22 March 2005

Kid Next Door!

Psychological warfare
With a six-year-old
You cannot win!
Football at my door
Stones even!
Swinging from your door cover
Get me out of here…
Psychological warfare
You can't win
You can't touch him
That's not me anyhow!
A fucking six-year-old…
You can't swear
His mother has a go!
Little brat…
Warfare
With a six-year-old
Fuck!

22 March 2005

Live For Today?

Many song lyrics say…
Live for today
Forget tomorrow!
I myself have two credit cards
Lucky me?
But tomorrow I have the bill
I'm all for…
Live for today!
But tomorrow does come…

22 March 2005

Jesus Guy?

Let's get this straight
I don't think…
I'm Jesus Christ from heaven!
Like Ian McCulloch
Bono
And many others…
I'm a Jesus guy!
Which is…
Someone who shines a light
The difference being…
My light shines through the stars
Like magic!
You tell me…

22 March 2005

Innocent

Up until a couple of years ago
I was innocent
I knew what I was writing, oh yes
But I never believed it was of any consequence
They still try to tell me…
It's all in my imagination (the illness)
Sorry! It's gone too far
But what's gone too far?
I'm still a nobody…
Am I?

23 March 2005

In the Clouds

My daughter tells me…
That when Christ comes back
He is going to take all the Christians
Up in the clouds…
Well, if I'm Christ or not
I believe…
My daughter
Is already in the clouds!
Which is fantastic!
Good luck to her…
What about
You and me…?

30 March 2005

Never Give In

If you're having a crap time
And your spirits are low
Never give in!
Remember…
When you're low
The only way is up!
But if you just keep getting lower
You just may break through.
That's when the pain becomes your friend…
The worst feeling
Is when you feel nothing
Pain is better than nothing
Have a tear
Have a wank
Never give in…

30 March 2005

In the Clouds

Slow Down

Eight years…
My first folder
1980 – '88
Three months
Two folders
2005
Slow down man!
Where's the fire?
Piss on it!

30 March 2005

II.iii

To the Devil a Daughter, 2005

Who's Laughing?

Life is a joke!
Are you in on the joke?

29 May 2005

To the Devil a Daughter!

There are many forms of love…
A daughter loves her daddy
No matter how!
And the dad loves her
So much!
The Devil can be the mother…
Life hurts us all
To the Devil a daughter!

29 May 2005

Strawberry Fields Forever

End of May 2005
Spring Bank Holiday
Strawberry Fields…
Come on!
MeMe Natalie and I
Not Poppy

Sky Walker!
Don't forget Sky Walker...

29 May 2005

No Gold?

End of May
Plan A.
Still no gold
Shove it up your ass
In little pieces
Your round table...
Plan B.
Jimmy Dean
On the cover of a magazine...

29 May 2005

Sunglasses After Dark

Still waiting?
World War Three.
Wake up!
Open your eyes
World on fire!
Get it?

29 May 2005

DNA

There it was!
All the time!
In my face...
LOVE...
DNA.

Breaking the code?
Fire!
SOS
No wonder…
Jack-in-the-box
Thank you one and all
Not!
Time to break the circle
The Browns…
Fuck!
Die!
Motherfuckers!
Just die…

30 May 2005

Puppet on a String

Pinocchio wishing he were a boy
A real boy…
God needs a laugh…
And so kept the strings
But turned him into
Captain Scarlet
Still wishing…
Cut those apron strings
Forty-five years!
Pinocchio gets his wish
A real boy!
No strings…
Only thing?
A boy needs a girl
A real girl
True and faithful
Soft and gentle
But today!
'Tomorrow'
Never comes…
Even trees

Need love
And a sick bucket…

31 May 2005

Uncle Colin

Uncle Colin
Pissing on the fire…
Always pissing?
You!
Your mates…
Always pissing
Taking the piss
USA
Bush
Come on!
Uncle Colin
Always pissing!

31 May 2005

Fear

Once you have mastered the fear of dying
You master the fear of living!
Hey I'm alive
Ready to die…

31 May 2005

The Mission

So many doubts
So many put-downs
I have always believed

5 September 2006

Where?

Where?
Where do you begin
Begin to start over?
Not only the fool!
But the fool everybody now knows
And penniless…
They lead you up the garden path
Just to push you
In a cowpat or two
The dawn?
Oh yes!
Dawn of the flies
Get it?
Bull SHIT!
All of it…

31 May 2005

All or Nothing

Look at the dates
Why so many?
Thirty-first May
If a Man
Has not got his word
What has he got
You all know
My poem
With its deadline…
How many times
Have you heard me say?
All or nothing
OK?
The world will spin and spin
We've all seen…
The movie
Pulp Fiction

We're all made of rubber
Come on shag me!
When I pop
I pop!
Adios amigo
Thirty-first of fucking May 2005…

31 May 2005

Always

On my own
Still…
MeMe
Pretending she likes me
Bullshit!
Just motivation
More crap poems…
Always
On my own…
Fuck Fuck
Fucking!
Always
Alone…
I never say to myself
What if?
I do try
God takes the piss
Julie
MeMe
I always try
But still
Alone…

31 May 2005

Brave New World

The birds are a singing…
First June 2005

The dawn chorus
And I feel fine!
One thing is your freedom
Another is to appreciate it…
So many are still prisoners
Maybe?
But little girl…
You have my beating heart
In your hands
Be gentle with me
Brave new world…
Come on!
Catch your breath
Let's go…

1 June 2005

Christian Music

New Christian music?
Psychobilly
Reverse psychology
You don't know a good thing
Till you've tasted the bad…!
1950s sci-fi
is twenty-first-century psychobilly
New Christian music!
Roll on…

1 June 2005

Titanic

We've all seen…
James Cameron
Titanic
Well?
My whole life
I've been looking for the stone
Again, well?

Like the old lady
I had it all the time…
It's not about owning the stone!
It's about the trip
The testimony
Pick a shoulder?
Best foot forward
Let's go…

1 June 2005

The Door is Locked!

Sorry my friend
Find another…
The door is locked!

7 June 2005

Ego?

We all have our egos
We all feed our egos
Where do you draw the line?
Egos?
Fucking egos
Come on…

8 June 2005

The Key…

Be gentle…
Turning my key
Heaven?
Heaven is for everyone
Spirits
Having flown…

8 June 2005

Open Your Eyes

The Christians
At my daughter's church
Are full of life!
They buzz with spirituality
And obviously they wish to share…
The buzz
But what they don't get
Don't understand…
Is that most
Already do have and enjoy
The very same buzz…
Open your eyes…
It's called?
…being alive

16 June 2005

All Pissed Out

Most of my life
I've been
Pissing on the fire!
All pissed out
Nothing left…
Empty!
What do you get?
Not a thanks…
Nothing!
Life?
Takes the piss
Just takes!

17 June 2005

Welcome to Hell!

Graffiti…
'Welcome to hell'
They ain't wrong!
Dragged here!
Kicking and screaming
Models…
Dolly birds
But here…
The hounds of hell!
The Devil's own…
Welcome to hell!

17 June 2005

Never Take Me Alive

Kirk Brandon
Me ol' buddy
Sings…
'Never take me alive'
Just to be wanted
Would be a start
Never take me alive
No one would notice!
Ninety-five mph
I felt the tyres move
Never take me alive
You're having a laugh…

17 June 2005

Three Wishes

It's in my face…
How lucky I am
Fuck you!

Fuck you one and all
Three wishes?
I wish, I wish, I wish
I were dead!
How simple do you want it?
DEAD!

17 June 2005

Doormat

Pissed off!
Indeed…
My 'LIFE' my stupid poems
Ripped off all the time
An idea?
A original thought?
Days, even hours later!
On TV in the media
Doormat
Walked all over
Where's me millions?
Sorry!
Just a doormat

18 June 2005

Me and Jacko

The whole world knows…
Wacko Jacko
Not a cent to his name
And free to go…
The whole world knows…
Me
Not a penny to my name
But free to go…
Get it?

19 June 2005

Blackout

A personal problem
Only I can sort out?
Or maybe not?
My trip to hospital
Pendered East, Northampton
The Mental Health System…
Why?
Mum and Dad…
Blackout!
You took my life
And gave me this
Why?
How can I forgive?
What I don't understand…
Blackout?
What did they do?
Blackout…

19 June 2005

All of Me?

All of me!
Why not take?
All of me…
Flat on my back
Arms wide open
All of me?

22 June 2005

Do You Dream?

I once owned…
A goods train
The day I got my Intercity 125

The earth ran out of fuel
All my life...
I dreamt of the Lottery
The day I won
They decided to do without money
Do you dream?
It ain't worth the wait...

27 June 2005

Out of the Blue

Asking myself again...
Anything unusual
In my childhood?
Well?
When I was ten, maybe eleven?
Walking in my village
Out of the blue!
From the sky...
A bolt of light
I was looking up...
It hit me
This light
No bullshit!
No big deal...
I don't remember telling anyone
It was the start of a storm
Out of the blue
No big deal...

28 June 2005

Too Safe...

My worker said to me
'Colin
'You like it safe?'
I've known this man
Twenty years!

And he said ‘safe’
Where has he been
What planet is he on?
Safe?
I live on the edge
Out there!
Obviously!
On my own…

28 June 2005

Contradiction

Life?
Life itself
Is a contradiction…

1 July 2005

G8 (Bandwagon)

It was said…
On the BBC *Question Time*
A couple of weeks ago
Pop stars
Should stay out of politics
What planet are they from anyway?
Well?
Pop stars are from earth…
Open your eyes!
What planet…
Do politicians live on?
It ain’t earth!
G8
Open your eyes!
Come on…

2 July 2005

Who Do You Think You Are?

Africa?
Africa at war…
Who are we?
To tell Africa
Sixty years ago!
Only…
Millions killed in Europe!
How long ago?
Northern Ireland…

2 July 2005

Around the Corner

All my life…
My living memory
I've been led to believe
It's just around the corner
What's around the corner?
Even today!

3 July 2005

Dancing to the Radio

Many years ago…
I would dance and bop
To the radio
Grafton Lodge
Northampton
The eighties
I wasn't some hippy
Saying…
'Give me the drugs'
I would dance and bop
Fighting the shit!

I never did want your drugs
Of course!
The more I danced
The more drugs
Needles all over the place
No choice
Dancing to the radio…

3 July 2005

Information

'The Mental Health System'
Making people well?
Maybe?
Maybe not?
Drugs?
Different trips
What does what?
Information!
That's my opinion
Couple of body bags
Why?
Information…

3 July 2005

A Promise

All those years ago…
A promise!
I've kept mine
I've delivered
No more looking away…
A promise…
Come on!

3 July 2005

How Many?

Sunday, Sunday
Looking for a poem…
Five-hundred plus!
How many do you want?

3 July 2005

II.iv

July 2005

Speck of Sand…

1984, Northampton
I was young
I believed I could make a difference
Africa…
World poverty!
Do I feel any different?
A few poems
Jesus? Even
We only see…
What they want us to see
That box
We call the TV
Lost interest?
I don't know
I just feel helpless…

5 July 2005

Too Many

Too many…
Don't know who?
Or where they're from.
If you know
Who you are
It may help you on your way.
If you don't know
Who you are –

Come on Mums and Dads
Sort it out!
Too many…

8 July 2005

Millionaire Poet

Have you ever heard of…
A millionaire poet
A dead one even?
Look out!
Stand back!
I'm a coming through
The first
Millionaire!
Rules?
Fuck the rules!

11 July 2005

Goo Goo Muck

Have you heard the song
Made famous by the Cramps
'Goo Goo Muck?'
Well I'm a fat old git
In my mid forties
But still very much a teenager…
Which makes me a goo goo muck!
Take
Elvis
Jim Morrison
Gene Vincent
It gets us all…
That weight gain
But hey!
I'm still rockin'

I'm your typical
Goo Goo Muck

11 July 2005

The Answer

Being alive
And being
Talking about it
On a worldwide scale
A homeless person
Has the same as a millionaire
Alive
And being
We all know all this
The electric
The human…
But who talks about this?
No one
Well!
When we start talking
It's the answer
Being alive
And being

12 July 2005

The Lotto

A friend of mine says…
She is deluded with the Lotto
She's deluded
Because she has not won yet!
Well I think…
She is deluded
Deluded if she thinks she is gonna win
I put my pound on…
Deluded I'm not
Fourteen million to one

But I do…
Put me pound on

12 July 2005

Religion

It's put in your head
As a kid
Just a child
When you're a man
We all know that it doesn't matter
Just an excuse for a fight
'Religion'

12 July 2005

The Bungalow

Talking with friends
Complaining about the Bungalow
Same old story
One said…
Wouldn't you like
A big smile and welcome?
My reply…
No, I reckon the staff feel sad
What does Colin want here?
Get it?

12 July 2005

Revolution

When they say…
Don't write love songs
Write about the 'Revolution'
Up the Revolution!
Don't you get it?

The Revolution…
Is the love songs!
If it ain't love
What?

13 July 2005

Speck of Sand #2

News at Ten…
More suicide bombers
Ten or more kids
Iraq
Who do I think I am?
A million silly poems
Just don't do it!

13 July 2005

Suicide Bombers

I don't know the politics
Suicide bombers…
How great must be the cause?
Forget the promise of heaven!
Christ what's happening?
Fuck?

13 July 2005

Unexplained

1980
Diagnosed Skitzo!
Twenty-five years explaining myself
'Me poems'
They now decide…
I'm not Skitzo
What about those…

That can't explain
Filled with drugs and shit
ECT?
Twenty-five years explaining
Something so simple
Back off Doc.
Shove it
We don't need it
And never did...

17 July 2005

Life in Progress

Nobody wants...
An unfinished work
That's why...
Poets are poor
It's a lifetime's work
'Life in progress'
An advance £££
Maybe?

17 July 2005

Rejected

A trip to Oxford
Pick up me poems
Rejected by the OUP
Their loss
Like the Byrds' song
'Turn, Turn, Turn'
My poems
Will have their day!

17 July 2005

No Mirrors

My poems are simple
Once you click on
Loads of mirrors
Reverse psychology
Contradictions…
No mirrors?

17 July 2005

My Vision?

I have always had this vision
Peace on earth…
One world, etc, etc
Where did it come from…
Was I born with it?
We are still a very long way off!
Is my book the vision?
Or maybe part of passing it on…
When writing a poem…
I try to be original
Just to find out later
I'm not!
The vision is also about attitude
A good attitude
With a touch of rebel
My vision
Was I born with it?

18 July 2005

My Vision #2

I am greatly inspired by music
And the lyrics in music
In this mixed-up world

I often feel I had inspired them
The vision…

18 July 2005

Spirits

Lifegate Baptist Church
Corby
I attend
Now and again
Spirits?
Something…
Makes my left side go stiff
Trying to enter
I'm not afraid, no
They don't feel friendly but
Every time…
Spirits
Something?
Lifegate Baptist
Corby

18 July 2005

Loaded

All my life
I have dreamt
Of riches
Spiritually
I'm loaded
What money can't buy
We only have the one life
If I am to be loaded
Come on…
I'd like to enjoy it
Today!

18 July 2005

Freedom…

Some
Haven't the grace
To enjoy their freedom
Some
Don't understand?
When you click…
Be careful
Freedom?
It can blow your mind

18 July 2005

Freedom… #2

Jesus…
Was about setting people free
The Church…
Is about controlling people
Fuck?
Jesus is the church
Isn't He?

18 July 2005

Driving in My Car

Brakes are for…
The accidents you can see
Seat belts…
The accidents you don't!

18 July 2005

Where Were You?

When I was a young man
I believed Jesus
To be a bastard!
Because He had written a book
The Bible, with such stories
That no one could follow
But now I realise
It was the Church that wrote the Bible
And the Church don't want anyone to follow
When you work it out!
The second coming…
Will be a man with such balls
He will just cut the crap!
Not unlike Jesus himself
When they crucified Jesus
He didn't die for my sins
I was on the cross with him!
Where were you?

18 July 2005

The Clever Bit

This vision of mine
Is really so simple
The clever bit
Is showing me it
My music
The TV
I've always had this vision
But still
They turn it over
That's
The clever bit

19 July 2005

Democracy

We live in a democracy
Part of being in a democracy
Is having debates
But if you win all your debates
That makes you a dictator
It isn't always about winning
Is it?

19 July 2005

Rubbed Off…

OK?
They tell me…
I'm not skitzo no more
I always knew that…
But?
A lifetime of pills
And shit…
Everyone telling me
I'm crazy…
A lifetime!
I ask you?
What now?

19 July 2005

More Than a Feeling

I have never been told what to write
What did happen…
I was always made to feel…
I was the one!
People walking by
Real voices
Then the music!
The TV

But again!
Real voices
Do you understand?
More than a feeling…

19 July 2005

Bang! Bang!

America
Kids with guns
Making that step
From child to man
Switches
Lights flashing
One slips the net…
Bang! Bang!
Everybody's dead
America…

20 July 2005

Big Days

I'm famous
But not famous
These are my big days…
Life is a blast!
Maybe I will be famous?
Maybe not?
I'll always remember
Big days!

20 July 2005

Same Time

Life?
Life is nothing

Life is everything
All at the same time
Life?
Life is a joke
Life is hard
All at the same time
Life?
Why…
Why not…
All at the same time
Child…
Adult…
And back again
All at the same time

22 July 2005

It Is Real…

It?
Whatever it is in your life
It is real!
All my life
I have been put down
Told I was crazy
I knew different
Now?
Now I'm telling you!
It?
It is real!
And always was

22 July 2005

The Third Word

Jesus had a vision
A world vision
Also a vision of heaven
Me, myself
A similar vision

Moving it along…
The Third word
A thousand years from now
Will be everything!
It will not be written…
From desire
The promise of riches
It will be written
Just because
It should be written
Watch and wait
The Third word
Will be…

24 July 2005

A Sad Day

A sad day…
I sit and watch the Lotto!
Why?
Promises
Pie in the sky
Me pound in
Not much else to do
A sad day…
The Lotto!
I've done me book
What more?

24 July 2005

In-joke?

'The Bible'
An in-joke…
Maybe?
I myself believe in Jesus!
What I don't believe is his press
Those stories…
No one will never know…

What another believes
And never will
'Coz…
They could be lying
When saying
In-joke…
Maybe?

25 July 2005

The Lonely Lighthouse

I sit here
Writing me poems
Shining me lights
The Lonely Lighthouse
Ships, people walk by
The lighthouse shines
Rocks
Love on the rocks
Still I shine
Writing me poems
Seasick…
I know

25 July 2005

Breaking the Code

A to Z
ABC
The English language
Any language?
Learning to read and write
It's about…
Breaking the code
A to Z
ABC
Up a tree…

25 July 2005

Asking Myself

Asking myself
Love?
Me with my hundred love poems
Why where when
If?
If at all
Maybe I've had my share?
Sorry boy that's ya lot
Asking myself
Love?
To sing a song...
Roll in the hay?
This day...

25 July 2005

Metaphors

The Bible
Is a book full of metaphors
Which means...
It can mean nearly anything
If you're gonna twist it
Why not...
Write your own?

25 July 2005

Give the Devil His Due

Love him?
Hate him?
Give the Devil his due
Without him?
You Christians
Wouldn't have a job

26 July 2005

II.v

August 2005

Your Drugs!

Not skitzo
Twenty-five years!
What was it then?
Listen here!
Drug addiction!
Set on fire…
Prescription drugs
Going apeshit…
As it kicks in
Cold turkey!
Up and down…
Schizophrenic then?
No you fool!
Your drugs…
Your damn drugs!
That's all it ever was…
Words just don't say what you have done…
Twenty-five years!
My life…

5 August 2005

Fire of Love…

Never told a thing…
The facts of life!
The birds and bees
That first trip to hospital
What was happening?

No one explained
Set on fire…
By love
Dad never told me!
Now?
Sorry Dad!
Too late…

5 August 2005

That Magic Space

Look up and down!
And around…
Have you noticed?
That magic space
The triangle
That spot
That spot
Between the eyes
Magic!
Get it?

5 August 2005

Infinity

If infinity goes on and on
Out!
Above and beyond…
Look inside?
Infinity again…
On and on
The mind
The void…
Infinity!

5 August 2005

Ungrateful

Medication…
Ungrateful am I?
Years of work…
Ungrateful am I?
I will never know…
And you can't tell me!

5 August 2005

Mentally Ill

OK?
I give in
I am mentally ill
Mentally ill…
In a mentally ill world
So?
Does that make me…
Normal
No! No!
No more arguing
Mentally ill…
That's me!
What more do you want?
You win
Mentally ill…

7 August 2005

I Dared!

So many in hospital
Have their 'Jesus' moment
I dared to explain
The fool that wrote it down
It's the drugs!

That's all it ever was…
I dared!
What did you?

7 August 2005

Stand Up!

Come on Christ!
Stand up…
So I can go down on my knees
Get on with my life!
Just like…
The sheep you all are
Baa… baa…

7 August 2005

Misunderstood / Elephants

I'm not misunderstood
You all know what I'm saying
Do you want me to lie?
Be a liar
Misunderstood I don't think so
Boring maybe?
Elephants?
I'll tell you about elephants!

7 August 2005

How Long?

Forever is a long time…
How long?
This love of mine
Forever is a long time…
How long?
The Farmhouse

Forever?
I haven't got forever
My love…

8 August 2005

Where?

Bluebirds may fly over the rainbow
Lovers, love under the moon
But lover where are you?
In my arms you aren't
My heart beats for you…
And you alone!
Bluebirds sing this song
For you and I
But where?
Step out of my dreams
Into my loving arms
Where are you?

8 August 2005

Come On Down!

Hey Jesus!
The great Jesus Christ!
Come on Man…
Step out of the clouds!
Me, myself?
I've done all I can
So OK?
I ain't Jesus
Come on Man…
This I've got to see!
My daughter
Tells me…
Hey! I'm holding my breath…

8 August 2005

Did I Miss It?

The Second Coming!
Did I miss it?

8 August 2005

Dear Natalie

Natalie my dear
If you lived ten life times
You would still be waiting
Jesus in the clouds?
I don't think so…
This may be my opinion but
You're missing out on so much!
But who am I to say?
Sitting in my flat, bored…

8 August 2005

These Silly Poems…

Nothing better to do…
Than write these silly poems
When am I going to find her?
The Girl
The Woman
The Love
They say don't go looking…
OK! I'm not looking
These silly poems…

8 August 2005

Band Aid

Easter 1984
St Crispin's, Northampton
Two young doctors
Wish to interview me
First thing I say!
Before we have even sat down
'Africa
We need to do something'
The doctors just leave
Say nothing
BAND AID?
Did that kick start Band Aid?
Hey! I'm mental
Put yourself in my shoes
A million things like the above?
Wouldn't you be crazy?

8 August 2005

All These Things

Nearly every day
Things happen…
Someone will say something
I may write a poem
Or say something
And things happen…
Coincidence?
Not every day
A million things
The Truman Show?
Come on?
Get real…
All these things…
And more!

8 August 2005

The Trip?

Years of pills
Needles…
Where did I go?
The trips?
The idea
I went to the idea
Imagine…
Being given a truth drug
Then left on your own
The answer we're all looking for
Is so simple
It's the idea
…in the idea

9 August 2005

Demons

Demons?
I have no demons
I sleep!
When I sleep
Water?
That may be a demon of mine
When I sleep
I breathe under water
Control your fears
Demons?
I have none

9 August 2005

Demons

Pennies from Heaven?

Kingswood/Lincoln, Corby
Pennies everywhere
Great Oakley
None
Ask yourself
Why do people in Great Oakley have money?
I may be missing the point!
But you have to start somewhere

10 August 2005

Magic in the World?

Not depressed!
But slowing down…
Magic?
Yes I believe in magic!
Things you cannot explain?
More human than heavenly…
Two years high in the clouds!
Coming down…
I even convinced myself there's a heaven
You tell me…
Magic?
Oh yes!
Magic in the world…

10 August 2005

Maybe I Am the One?

Natalie tells me…
Christ is going to step out of the clouds!
Well?
I've been in the clouds for years…
Maybe I am the one?

11 August 2005

My Poems…

My poems ain't about…
Clever educated poetry
I can't even spell
It's about a vision
From start to finish
The vision is in every line
It's not clever
I'm not even educated
I have a vision…
Come!
Share the vision
My poems…

11 August 2005

Dust and Drugs

We are all bits of dust
From the earth, OK?
So plants and veg
Are also bits of dust from the earth
The earth being…
The Mother!
Drugs are also chemicals
From the earth
So what's the big deal about drugs?
It's all dust from the Mother
Drugs?
Drugs are the future
The Bible tells me so…
But not a preacher
Come on…
Catch up

11 August 2005

Unknown

Being unknown…
Has its advantages
I can write exactly what I want!
Being a pop star
You have to fit the schedule.
My big disadvantage
No money!
No pat on the back…

11 August 2005

Heaven or Hell?

Some say…
When you die
There is a light!
Head for the light.
This may be a contradiction
For the light must be the sun
A ball of fire!
They say hell is a lake of fire.
Life is all contradictions!
Looks like?
Death is also…
Heaven and hell…
Will we ever know?
It may be too late when we do.

11 August 2005

Two Fish

G8, Edinburgh
A million people
Did I miss me moment?
Well? No…

I haven't much to say
It's all in me book
A million people?
Two fish
Come on!

11 August 2005

Not Asking!

When I ask a question
It's not really a question
More of a statement
When I say to people
'What's it all about?'
I'm not asking!

11 August 2005

All or Nothing!

When I make up my mind
It's all or nothing
So if you're coming with me
All or nothing!
When she said, 'I do'
And two years she was gone
Now it's nothing
Forever on my own
So if you're looking at me
Remember…
All or nothing!

14 August 2005

Enjoy the Trip

Forget your millions
Start enjoying yourself

Enjoy the trip!
I have always enjoyed myself
Even at my most depressed
It's all in my head!
The music!
Real or unreal?
It's a blast!
Dance!
Motherfucker…
Enjoy the trip!

15 August 2005

Let It Go…

Let it go…
No one's interested
They've got their own lives
Let it go…
Your poems?
It's not important
The answer?
Who cares

15 August 2005

Only an Image

The Devil…
Gave us rock and roll
Why?
To inspire 'The One'
The Devil
Wants to be saved like us all
The Devil
Is misunderstood
Music?
Only an image

15 August 2005

The Holy Spirit

God the Father
God the Son
God the Holy Spirit
The Holy Spirit
Is what joins us all together!
The human race…
When you were a kid
Did you ever limp at a corner?
Just to find a man limping
The Holy Spirit
Can be magical
When we help one another
The Holy Spirit
That's what I see…
You tell me?

17 August 2005

Interpretation

My daughter asked me…
'Do you think you are the Jesus in the Bible?'
My reply…
'My interpretation, yes!'
Also I said…
'Who has the right interpretation?'
I didn't ask for the drugs
They made me
Who I am
Read my words
Still nobody can say…
Interpretation?
Get it?

17 August 2005

Living the Blockbuster

Ask yourself
Is your life interesting?
Me, myself
I'm living the blockbuster
Read my words
They hardly touch it!
Even on my own
Listening to my music
It just doesn't stop!
The party…
Living the blockbuster!

17 August 2005

Discovered

When am I going to be discovered?
This poet…
This Jimmy Dean?
It's a game…
Everybody already knows me
Discovered?
It's a joke…
People look at me
Some talk and shake my hand
What's going on?
Jimmy Dean…
Where's the magazine?

17 August 2005

All My Love

They say…
Life is give and take
How much?

Six million poems?
Come on!
All my love?
You had that years ago…
The girl?
The motor…
All my love?
My love

17 August 2005

Comes in Threes

They say…
Things happen in threes
Comes in threes
Well?
Charles and Camilla wed
The Pope passed away
And…
I travelled to Oxford with me poems
April 2005
The first weekend in April
I was alive!
The spirit was strong
Magic in the air!
God bless you Charles!
John Paul's away
And I'm still a nobody…
Am I?

17 August 2005

The Waiting Game

Twelve years…
On my own
Mostly my choice
Got to a point
With my poems

Now looking!
First things first
The farm
The motor
This time!
Playing for keeps
No games
Twelve years
Alone
The waiting game

17 August 2005

II.vi

August–September 2005

Britney Spears?

If Britney Spears lived local
She would likely attend the Bungalow
Because…
She would think she were Britney Spears
Well?
I attend the Bungalow
Because…
I think I'm Colin Farquhar

19 August 2005

Paranoia

Paranoia can be mostly negative
They're out to harm you?
Get you?
My paranoia is fun
A million songs just for me!
Everybody's for me…
Go cat go!
Nice to meet you
Paranoia?
It's a laugh…

19 August 2005

Open Your Eyes

Twenty years ago…
I wrote a poem about my eyes
And what I could see!
Nowadays…
My music, the TV
People, real people
Say to me…
Open your eyes
What they don't understand is
My eyes are open
Life of Riley…
I don't think so
Open your eyes!

19 August 2005

Switch Off

I sit here writing me poems
Shining me lights
As I walk through the town
Those lights
My music
The TV
Switch off!
Let it go
You can only take so much
Fuck?
Some don't see a thing
Every day
Always…
The lights?

19 August 2005

Forever!

If I were to die tomorrow
Or in 300 years time…
I would have lived forever!
My forever…

19 August 2005

My Ideas

I don't watch much telly
Because…
When I do
I see my poems all the time
OK not the poems!
But the ideas in my poems…
And I'm sitting here on benefits
Frustrated…
But also when I don't see me poems
I'm saying
Where's me poems?
I can't win…
My poems
My ideas…

19 August 2005

Get a Life!

I need a change!
A girlfriend?
Seven poems today…
Why?
Nobody's reading them
Get a life!
Move town?
Start again…

Stevenage maybe?
Letchworth…
Too many ghosts
Get a life…

19 August 2005

Excalibur

Excalibur…
Returned to the lake
Could I have done more?
Excalibur…
In with the shopping trolleys
And dead fish
Excalibur…
Until the next time
The magic!
Excalibur…
My dear friend

20 August 2005

Melting Pot

Again it's the medication maybe?
Cold turkey…
Too much?
Many a night…
I have smelt my skin
Melting like fire
But if we come from the earth?
And the earth from the sun
Then we're made of fire anyway
Cold turkey…
Too much?
I'm on fire

21 August 2005

Biggest Fan?

If you're a pop star
Celebrity
Anyone famous…
Who's ya biggest fan?
The guy with the shotgun!
Blowing your brains out…
Shotgun…
Pop star?
Bang! Bang!
He's ya man…

22 August 2005

Let It Be…

You spend your life
Trying to work it out
What's it all about?
When you get there
You find…
You had it all the time!
If you do or don't find it
Let it be…
It's not important
Sadly you have to find it first
To believe

24 August 2005

Still Nowhere?

When I was first mentally ill
I was crazy
Going apeshit
Two-and-a-half decades later
Not much has changed

I have accepted my destiny
And learned self-control
I still have many of the thoughts and ideas
I had when I was twenty
Going ape gets you nowhere
I'm still nowhere
Maybe?

24 August 2005

Alive

Do you know
What it is like to be alive?
I mean so alive…
Not only to touch the flame
You are the flame!
No drugs!
Natural…
It's the only way
Then…
To pass it on
Fuck?
I've been there…
Alive!
So alive…

25 August 2005

The End?

Never had the time…
Rushing everywhere!
The future?
This big empty space
Never had a future…
The end?
Turned forty and a bit
All change…
Things are different!

All the time in the world
The end?
It's not important…

27 August 2005

Deflated

The Lotto?
Saturday night
Always a little deflated
I know the odds
My illness
It always misleads me
Never mind?
Next time…

27 August 2005

Is God Simply Paranoia?

There is a space in the mind
In between and just behind the eyes;
I call this 'the idea'.
I may be looking for God
But is God simply paranoia
Looking within?
When in church…
And the people are praying
I see them in this space within the mind
Tell me
Who are they praying to?
It's just a space…

29 August 2005

Spending My Time

I spend most of my time
In the idea

Drug-induced
Long-term medication…
Paranoia…
The fun side of paranoia
One voice
My voice…
Am I missing something?
Where's God?
He ain't talking to me
And I don't believe the Christians
Praying all the time…
Me?
Just a…
Spending my time

29 August 2005

This Spot

Many may not know what I'm talking about
This spot in the mind…
Mentioned in the last couple of poems
Good general education can bring you there!
Medication…
The misuse of drugs or alcohol
My daughter's pastor was an alcoholic
When he bangs his pulpit
I believe he as found the idea, the space
He likes to call it 'God'
I feel he is still looking
When preaching…
Who's he trying to tell?
Us or himself…
This spot
Paranoia?
I call it 'the idea'

29 August 2005

Stimulation

On my own...
A million CDs
I need stimulation
Simple R'n'R
Today's music
Pop!
On my own...
Pulling my hair out
Music?
It's an addiction
Stimulation...
Give it to me!

29 August 2005

Living the Dream

When I was a kid
I remember...
I always wanted to be Jesus!
Pop stars sing to me!
Jesus with attitude
King of Kings
Living the dream!
You can't tell me any different!
King of Kings...
Come on...

29 August 2005

H_2O?

The human body...
Is made partly with a lot of water
H_2O
Tell me...
What are clouds made of?

H_2O
So…
Maybe we do end up in the clouds
Watering the daisies…
H_2O?

29 August 2005

Self-Control

Being mentally ill
Is partly about self-control
Down the pub
Down the disco
Ain't the problem!
It's the quiet times
Not much happening
Bored…
Self-control
That's when it counts…

30 August 2005

Happy Birthday Son…

Fifteen today!
My dear boy
Happy birthday
What can I say?
Taken from me
All those years ago
I could have done more
I kinda didn't want to rock the boat
Being a yes man
The medication that is…
I could do more today
But I believe it's up to you now
If you want me?
Happy birthday son…

30 August 2005

In Too Deep!

I'm not in the real world
I think my poems are something
I'm lost in this dream world…
The farmhouse?
It's a joke
This trip I'm on…
Help!
In too deep!
And there's nothing I can do
This poem?
Just more of it!
Help?
Electric, pills…

1 September 2005

Find Me a Tree?

Suicide?
It doesn't solve anything
Life?
It's a laugh
100 mph?
Find me a tree

1 September 2005

One?

A million signs…
Flashing lights
You're the One!
Where's the man?
The backer
The business man!
One is a lonely number

One?
To take on the world…

3 September 2005

What's Your Sunday?

Sunday?
What's yours?
A walk to church
Relax with the papers
Me?
I'm a car booter
What's yours?

3 September 2005

Therapy

All these poems…
Self-therapy maybe?
Bestseller…
Therapy for others?
No! No!
I'm still messed up!
Therapy it ain't

4 September 2005

Spinning

We're all looking for answers
What's it all about?
Well?
I've found some of those answers
But even if…
I had all the answers
I still have to get on with my life
Fill the time

So being a smart ass
Ain't all it's cracked up to be
Those answers?
Ain't worth the bother…
My head…
Just keeps spinning
Why?
These poems…

4 September 2005

Get Away?

I sit here with a tear in my eye
In my little dream world…
Which is my whole life
Powerless to help myself
Trying to work it out
Not the answers to life…
But how to move on
Get away from this 'Jesus' thing
Fall in love, maybe?
Someone to believe in
Where?
Where do I start?

4 September 2005

Count Your Blessings

Living in India
A tin hut if you're lucky
It rains
And it's washed away.
The fantastic USA
No one gives a shit
I'm OK Jack!
If you've got the cash…
Here in the UK
The NHS

Benefits…
Count your blessings…

4 September 2005

The Cat Is Out the Bag

Years ago, back in the eighties
I was writing what was on my mind
I didn't think about the consequences
The knock-on effect
Nowadays…
The cat is out the bag
We have to grow up, sometime?
I knew what I was writing
I just didn't have an ending
Likely because there is no ending
I always believed I would be looked after
'God', call it what you like…
I like to think it is more of a human thing
And yes I am looked after!
Financially…
But with my independence
The cat is out the bag
Nowadays…
I know exactly what I'm writing
But still with no ending…

5 September 2005

At Your Feet!

I laid my life at your feet!
Twenty-five years!
No, forty-five, all of it!
Two carrier bags…
It came back in a box
Unwanted!
My life, not good enough?
My ideas

My dreams
All laid out in black and white
My destiny?
We're all somebody
My life…
At your feet
I'll show ya
Everyone knows me!
And so will you…

5 September 2005

Bitter

You make me bitter
Life makes me bitter
All these wonderful love songs…
Will no one save me?
Looking over the edge
Bitter?

5 September 2005

Watch Me Fly…

How many flying lessons does one need?
Let me go!
Watch me fly…
Your meds?
I know!
Christ come on…
Watch me fly?

5 September 2005

Life Is Worth More Than Gold

Life is worth more than gold!
But not in the USA

Hurricane Katrina
Martial law
Millions in misery
You shouldn't loot
But to be shot…

7 September 2005

Last Night in Church…

Tonight!
Lifegate, Corby
My last night in church!
You all know my poems
My ideas
Time to move on…
Fall in love?
Jesus knows who I am
Heaven?
We will see…
Time to move on…
Slow down maybe?
Find something new to write about
Let someone else be God?
Talking of God…
Come on Mac
Ya new album next week
I know
You know
Anyhow…
This was
My last night in church…

7 September 2005

Saint or Sinner?

Jesus Christ…
Saint or sinner?
It doesn't matter

It's the idea…
Believing in the idea
Get it?

8 September 2005

Liberator

Who is your liberator?
Music is mine!
Jesus?
Drugs?
My poems maybe?
Music!
Give it to me…

8 September 2005

II.vii

New Direction, 2005

Stick to Your Guns

Twenty years ago!
I wrote…
'Jesus walks in everyone…'
Stick to your guns!
If you believe in Jesus or not
It's the enlightenment…
When you get the enlightenment!
That's the second coming!
For everyone…
If you can't handle it?
That's OK
We have some pills
Get it?

19 September 2005

A Personal Thing

He isn't going to step out of the clouds
The second coming
It's a personal thing…
2K
It's in all of us
It's about feelings
Enlightenment…
Personal enlightenment
I'm not 'Jesus'
But I may be the one to point this out
2K
It's in all of us

19 September 2005

New Direction

Back in '87
Mac wrote his song…
'New Direction'
He may have been looking for God?
Well this is my poem…
'New Direction'
I want to forget that 'Jesus' stuff
Move on…
September '05
No more Jesus or God!
Ten days and counting…

19 September 2005

OPEC

Sucking the milk from the mother
Where do you start?
I don't want to give up my licence
The end…
When it really is the end
Everyone will be saying…
'It wasn't me…'

19 September 2005

Conspiracy Theory

9/11
Did the US do it themselves?
The Christians think they own the world
The ticket?
It gave them the ticket
To bomb the world…

19 September 2005

Rock Bottom

Rock bottom…
Doesn't have a bottom
You can always sink a bit lower
Believe me…
When you're down there, really down there
You find something…
You find yourself
And within yourself a freedom
Back with the living…
This freedom stays with you
Rock bottom…
Let's fly!

20 September 2005

Gateway

Many years ago I wrote…
'Let them in
Heaven or hell you decide'
Well if 'heaven' is in the idea
Some of us may be the gateway…
Things happen in my life
Quite bizarre…
Who knows?
Am I such a gateway…?

20 September 2005

Gateway #2

I also wrote the words…
'Disappear up your own'
Does this mean…
We are the gateway to our own heaven?
Heaven?

Idea or not...
If you don't believe
You ain't going nowhere

21 September 2005

Crucifixion

Believe me I do want to move on
Nine days and counting...
Christ gave the crowd their freedom
The crowd didn't have the grace to know what to do with it
So the crowd wanted him dead
That's how I see it!

21 September 2005

Down the Local...

If alcohol...
Is a way to God
Why does Pastor Pavitt...
Want to empty the pubs?
He found God...
At the bottom of a pint glass!

21 September 2005

Bullying

My boy Luke...
Was and maybe still is
A victim of bullying
Somewhere along the line
He found he could push
His younger brother around a little
Drew is a victim...
Of Luke's insecurities

I try to tell him…
But he's not listening

21 September 2005

Nicky

We met at three am
Lovers by four
A birthday party
This is Colin Farquhar
Was I the one?
Many a trip to A & E
A million stars walking home
Addington
And she was on fire!
In the paper a train accident
I asked
It wasn't her
Where is she now?
Looking for love
We're all looking for love

21 September 2005

Stigma

If I really did become someone
With my poems…
There would be the stigma
He's mental…
Schizophrenia?
Bipolar?
Manic?
It's all a laugh to me…
Stigma?
I haven't got a stigma
That's your problem…
Sort it out!

22 September 2005

Excited…

Excited…
Life is so exciting!
Going nowhere…
Excited!
Feel my pulse
I'm alive
Red blood
My blood…
The sun shines
The breeze blows
Life…
Excited!

22 September 2005

Drunk and Sober

One drunk one sober?
It doesn't work!
Our nights out…
Being the driver
A hundred conversations
We never had…
Down the local…
Coming home to the wife
It doesn't work!

22 September 2005

In the Spotlight

Abba sings…
'Super Trouper'
Those spotlights…
Sometime now!

How many poems do you want?
Give it to me…

22 September 2005

Stories

The Bible…
King Arthur and Excalibur
World War II
The Matrix…
Stories…
It's how they make you think and feel…
The enlightenment
Fact or fiction
It ain't important
It's today…
It's you!

22 September 2005

How Far Can Too Far Go?

The chancellor predicts 4 per cent
Increase in the economy
Why?
The Olympics
World record broken
How?
Chill out everyone!
We ain't going nowhere
Step back…

22 September 2005

Buzz Buzz A-Diddle It!

Rockabilly…
Psychobilly…

1981 that's the buzz!
Polecats…
Meteors…
It must be soon?
That big wheel a-turning

22 September 2005

Litter v Poetry

In the local paper
Picking up litter…
In the local paper
Our book of poetry…
Everyone saying about the litter
No one mentioned the poems
Litter v Poetry
The rubbish every time!

27 September 2005

Children of the Revolution

The world spins
A new sunrise every day!
Will they ever get it right?
Peace on earth…
The kids know!
Unfortunately we all grow up
The world spins
And always will…
With or without us…

27 September 2005

Let Down?

Did I let you all down?
Did I pass with flying colours?
I feel let down

No one said in my face, Yes!
A million lights!
How safe do I want it?
Did I miss my moment?
A bit down indeed…

28 September 2005

Goodnight…

Goodnight Jesus,
Goodnight Nan and Grandad
Jesus, I don't want to talk about you too much more
But I know you will always be there for me…
Nan and Pop, I love you so much!
I hope I haven't let you down?
Yes! I could see it in your eyes
I've done my book
What more?
Goodnight…

28 September 2005

The Rest of Your Life?

We all know what it is all about…
Sex!
Reproducing…
OK?
That's thirty minutes
What about
The rest of your life…?

1 October 2005

Fighting…

You don't have to be big and strong
It ain't big!

You have to have it in you!
To put your fist through somebody's face
Fighting ain't the answer
But sometimes…
I wish I had it in me!
Sometimes…

3 October 2005

Tell Your Kids…

For the record!
My illness…
What is it?
Being set on fire by love!
I was never told…
About the birds and bees
Then the meds…
They never said or asked a word
Drug addition!
You may think it's funny
But even today!
Tell your kids…

4 October 2005

Shaking of Hands

The people at my daughter's church
Always shake my hand
But we are shaking hands for different reasons
They shake my hand because
We believe in the Bible and Christian fellowship
Well?
I found Christ!
But not through the Bible
I found Him
Turning myself inside-out
Without the Church and its dictation
But!

Does my book then become the new dictation?
You can't win…

5 October 2005

Feeding the Monster…

There is a monster within me
Not evil or bad
But a monster just the same.
I get frustrated
And bored…
The monster needs feeding
New music!
With lyrics for his ego
Feeding the Monster…

6 October 2005

For Real…

Twenty-five years…
Writing these poems
A fiction writer?
Could have knocked it up in a couple of weeks
But this is my life!
I felt and experienced every word.
Whether you agree or not
I'm for real…

6 October 2005

To Be Or Not To Be?

The farmhouse!
To be or not to be?
Whether I live there or not?
It has done its job
Kept me going!

Gave me a goal…
Not a flower in the garden!
Waiting for me?
To be or not to be?
The *Ink-Shed* magazine volume three
Left out 'to be' in the line
'…the house was to be mine,'
Made me look a fool
I was never a fool…
To be or not to be?
We will see…

6 October 2005

Racist

This week in the Bungalow
I was told to stop saying racist jokes
Or I would be asked to leave
No way am I a racist!
But being told to stop the jokes
Made me out to be one
Political correctness?
Part of the job
Whatever…
I believe the member of staff
To be more of a racist
Than me…
At that moment

7 October 2005

Giving Up?

Giving up the Bungalow…
Is like giving up smoking
You keep trying!
Then it just happens
Is this it?

8 October 2005

It's

It's a song
It's a poem
It's the music
It's in front of you
It's inside you
It's all around
It's life
It's death
It's everything

8 October 2005

This Road

All through the eighties
I dreamt of a big win…
With 'Spot the Ball'
But did I?
At different times…
I had three marked coupons.
Deep down
I was on a mission,
A different road.
My book…
Is all but done.
The money…
Am I too late?
This road…
My choice?
You tell me!

9 October 2005

Insomnia?

Insomnia?
Bad thoughts…

Nightmares?
Life is fantastic!
The possibilities…
Turn it around!
It's all in your head
But still…
Insomnia!

9 October 2005

Dr Who?

We're all time travellers
With time machines
The watch on your arm
The clock on the wall…
Travelling…
Second by second into the future
Dr Who?
Dr you and me

10 October 2005

Free…

No more pushing elephants…
Up the stairs
No more crashing pianos
I'm free…
And always have been!

10 October 2005

Credit Where Credit's Due

All of my life
I have aspired to be…
Someone I know very little about
Jesus

I have turned myself inside-out
When all the time
It was only ever myself…
Many have shown the way
Turned on the lights
Had trips I would never have dared
So?
If my words set you free
Best wishes
Credit where credit's due

10 October 2005

All the Time in the World

Love?
When you have found love!
Not sex…
Not lust!
But love in your heart
You really do have…
All the time in the world

10 October 2005

II.viii

October, November 2005

Dig Myself a Hole

Politics?
A hundred words when ten will do
Room for misinterpretation
Too many words?
Too many poems?
Digging myself a hole?
At the conference
Wake up!
Time to go…
Do you dig graves?
Yer groovy man!

11 October 2005

For a Dollar!

My story –
Will it ever be told?
Your story –
Have you written it yet?
Hollywood blockbuster –
Is that you or me?
Stories
Just stories…
My story?
Entertainment
For a dollar!

11 October 2005

Who Am I? #Whatever

I live in England
I come from the working class
I have found freedom!
Or at least as free as a man can be.
I live on benefits
In a two-bedroom council flat.
I dream of the millions in the Lotto
Not unlike nearly everybody.
Sometimes I'm a prisoner of my own freedom
In a routine.
My music?
What can I say,
It's everything...
Who am I?
Read my book...
Someone who dared to dream...
And lives that dream.

11 October 2005

Who's Watching?

My so-called illness
Tells me that someone is watching me
Who?
The world...
You?
God!
Or just good old paranoia
It's almost like I'm watching a movie of myself
With the real me up in the back row
Who?

11 October 2005

The World Is Your Oyster…

You will never find…
A pearl in your oyster
Because…
You are the pearl
And the world…
Your oyster!

11 October 2005

Let Go?

How do I let go?
Stop even?
Or at least slow right down
These poems…
Maybe if someone took an interest
Agreed with a few
What am I trying to prove?
My very existence
Come on…
Let go?

11 October 2005

Dots

What are we?
The earth, everything…
Dots!
Zillions of dots
Atoms
Sorry, too technical
The air we breathe
Water?
Dots
Just dots!

11 October 2005

The Back of Love

Mac me old buddy sings
'Breaking the back of love'
But they never did...
Love may break you
But love itself
Can never be broken!
The eighties
In and out the hospitals
But now?
They have a bit more time...

12 October 2005

Democracy?

Democracy?
Ain't always about the majority
Or the little guy
Would never be heard
Tell me...
How does it work?

14 October 2005

In Heaven...

Sad or happy?
I'm in heaven...
And always have been
This body of mine
Insignificant
I'm told
Suicide is a sin...
I believe
When it's your time, it's your time!

16 October 2005

Back to Church?

Today Sunday!
I'm considering going to church
Not for dictation
But then it never was for me
But standing and singing
Closing your eyes for prayers
I myself believe in Jesus
But I don't believe in the Church
I have an hour to decide
I'm so alone…
But that shouldn't be a reason for going to church
Should it?

16 October 2005

World on Fire!

The world is on fire with lust and desire
And that is where they want you
They want your sweat
Many have the answers
But they don't want you to have the answer
Again, they want your sweat!
My words will set you free!
World on fire?
Someone has to move the shit…

23 October 2005

Let Sleeping Dogs Lie?

If as I say…
My words may set you free
Why then have I this great desire for…
Me millions?
If you are already free

My words may remind you…
If not?
Let sleeping dogs lie…

23 October 2005

Is This It?

Is this it?
My life…
Stuck at the end of Finland Way
New kitchen
New bathroom…
Is this all I'm worth?
Finland Way…

25 October 2005

Lonely

Missing the Bungalow…
What's the point?
The Bungalow!
Staring at the wall…
Looking for a CD
Stimulation?
TV?
Forget the TV
Not many visitors
And no one to visit…
Lonely…
Oh yes!
Lonely and alone…

25 October 2005

Sex Drive

Where has it gone?
Sex beat!

The pills…
Me age?
No sex drive!
No wank!
Maybe a good woman?
We'll see…

25 October 2005

Rubber Scissors

Mac me old buddy
Gave us…
'The Cutter'
So OK
I took the bait
But now!
He's gone and shoved 'em in the sand

25 October 2005

Who Needs It?

Roger at the Bungalow…
A writer
He needs it!
Take me?
I've seen within the fairytale
I've seen the beginning the end
It's not important
Me?
A writer…

26 October 2005

How Many Stories?

The Bungalow again…
The staff

How many stories?
How many lies?
And how long?
The crap I've heard just recently…
What can I say?

26 October 2005

The Straight and Narrow

We all know life…
With its contradictions
Life is a contradiction!
Well, there is this place…
The straight and narrow
Boring I hear you say
But listen!
It's magic…
It's not always about being goody-good
Look within
The straight and narrow

1 November 2005

Walk that Walk

Nobody can touch you…
Walking the straight and narrow!
Sadly there's always one…
No grace!
Walking the walk…
You see life from a different angle
Life is a blast!
You see the funny side
Come on, what you waiting for?
Walk that walk…

1 November 2005

Can You Feel It?

We all know the song…
'Love Is in the Air'
Well?
If you believe in Jesus
The love in the air
May well be spiritual.
I myself…
Feel comfort in the space around me
Love is in the air?

1 November 2005

Is God Paranoia?

When things happen…
Coincidences?
My daughter would say…
No! that's God
I suffer from paranoia
Things happen to me all the time…
What I'm saying is…
Is God simply paranoia?

1 November 2005

What If?

What if…
The Bible ain't about Jesus at all?
What if…
The Bible ain't about the past?
What if…
The Bible is you and me today?
Crucifixion…
Fuck?

Life is for living!
Today…

6 November 2005

What If? #2

OK the Bible
You and me today…?
Death?
The gateway to a better life
But first!
You must prove yourself…
Crucifixion…
Do you have the faith?
Death?
Have you the faith?

6 November 2005

Demons and Devils

Why do I listen to…
Psychobilly music?
Demons and devils…
If I am to save a kid or two
I have to know
What from…
And for myself…
Listening to something quite sick
Inspires me to be good!
Demons and devils…
Come on!

31 October 2005

Misunderstood

If you're of an age
Forty-ish say…

How many times did you hear it said:
'If Jesus were here today
They would put him in a mental hospital'?
Well?
In my opinion…
They did just that!

15 November 2005

Blowing in the Wind

You all know my poems…
You may not think so
But it's in all of us!
Blowing in the wind
N E W S
Always was and will be…

19 November 2005

Stand Up!

Stand up!
I hear you say…
Hey!
I'm standing
What do you want?
Fire?
Well?
Piss on it…
I'm standing

19 November 2005

Every Way is South

King of the mountain?
King of the world…
Standing on the top of the world

Every way is south…
High road?
Low road…
It's all south
Let's go!

19 November 2005

Steps

Step by step
Always moving forward
A crossroads?
Onwards and upwards
Signpost
Bright lights
Maybe one more hill
A forest?
The stars
The magical moon
Do you lead?
Do you follow
Steps…
Let's go

19 November 2005

Did I Miss Something?

Walking along
Hands in pockets
Head down
Nowhere to go
Walked over my horizon
The skies are blue
Hands in pockets
Head down
A few steps more…
Did I miss something?

19 November 2005

Ask Alice

I look in the mirror
Yes that's me!
I play a CD or two
I reminisce
I remember some crazy things
Ideas…
What's reality?
What's mental illness?
Ask yourself…
Is that you?

19 November 2005

When?

When does a rebel…
Stop being a rebel?
In his box
Pushing up daises…
A family
To bring up?
A bad person
Ain't always a rebel
Being a rebel
Is more about being cheeky
So…
When does a rebel?
Stop rebelling

20 November 2005

Until…

Walk away?
Nowhere to walk…
If you want me?

Show me the way
I have the key…
Until then
Until…

20 November 2005

Who's Watching? #2

I feel as if I'm being watched
Big Brother maybe?
Is it what the Christian's call
Born again…?
With God watching!
Paranoia?
Self-enlightenment…
When you turn this corner
You can't help yourself…
You have to try to behave
Is it you?
Is it yourself…
Who?

20 November 2005

Another Christmas…

A bit colder this year!
But still…
Another Christmas!
Have you been good?
Makes no odds
When you don't have a loved one
Another Christmas…

20 November 2005

Christmas Cards?

Some say:
Why send Christmas cards
When you don't get in touch any other time...?
Well?
When would you get in touch?
Without...
Christmas!

20 November 2005

Boy Blue...

I very well may be Boy Blue
With all my poems!
But who knows about 'em?
One day!

20 November 2005

II.ix

If Not Now? 2005

Slapping It About!

There is this guy…
I think they call him 'Red'?
Not Red from Blissworth!
Anyhow
He likes the ladies
And the ladies like him!
One day
He is going to be sad, old and lonely
With a disease or two…
Oh yes!
He knows what it's all about…
But does he?
When he's ready to settle down
No girl will want him!
Hey stupid!
You just can't help yourself!
Slapping it about…

24 November 2005

Moving On?

All my many breakdowns
I have put it behind me
Moved on…
This time
I can't let it go!
It's gone too far…
They promise you the world!

This time I want it
This time…
But what if…
It is all in my head?
Then it's all a lie
My life
My poems
Everything!
Moving on?
I want to, I need to
But
Not this time!
Not yet…

24 November 2005

For Me?

Nan and Grandad…
Sitting by the coal fire
Watching a black-and-white TV
Myself…
With me headphones on
Full of life!
Big hopes for me…
Art college
The Jam *This is the Modern World*
Nan picking Brussels at six a.m.
Fingers red frozen!
She never complained
What do I know?
It was all there…
Shining in their eyes
Nan and Pop
All for me…

24 November 2005

An Angel for Me?

Is my luck a-changing?
Rock 'n' roll
The British Railway Club
Tonight!
An angel came down from heaven
A dance, maybe two
The prettiest girl of them all!
Brown eyes
A full bosom
An angel…
My luck, it must be a-changing?
Please, please
We will see!
Take your time
An angel indeed…

25 November 2005

Two Kinds of People

They who know!
And they who don't
It's about feelings
'A born-again Christian'
Ain't just words…
Myself?
I'm a born-again Colin.
But when did this happen?
Them and us?
There are those who know but don't realise they know
Those who know and just get on with it!
Some don't know and never will
Two kinds of people
Them who know!
And them who don't
But it ain't that simple
Enlightenment?

The big picture…
Who cares?
Before you ask!
You must know what you're asking
Still…
Who cares?
Them who know?
Them who don't?
And does it make a difference?

26 November 2005

Never-ending Story

They who know!
And they who don't
It doesn't end!
Because no one knows what another is thinking
And new people, i.e. babies
Are born every day!

27 November 2005

Delta City/Dreamtime

We've all seen *Robocop*!
With 'Delta City'
Well?
Look up the Cult album…
Dreamtime
Because that's my hometown at the moment!
Track one, 'Horse Nation'
I've seen it coming!
And waited for ever
Corby!
Don't blow it

27 November 2005

One Day?

Morrissey has a live DVD
Entitled
Who Put the 'M' In Manchester?
One day
I'd like it said…
'Who put the C in Corby?'

27 November 2005

Magical World?

The wind in the trees
The air we breathe
Waves crashing on rocks
The water we drink
Love…
The mystery that is lovemaking
Magical world?
Oh yes!

27 November 2005

Directions

Someone stops you!
And asks directions
You know exactly where it is!
But you have to pass on the information
What I'm saying is
'I have a vision'
But have I passed it on?

27 November 2005

Be True My Love

Sitting in the jungle at midnight
A thousand eyes!
Like the stars in the night sky…
A thousand eyes?
A thousand stars?
Be true my love…

27 November 2005

Isolation

They who know!
And they who don't
Those who know!
But believe they're on their own
I believe this can be a contributor to mental illness
It's about…
Making the switch
I was on my own
And you all know my history
800 poems…
About nothing?

28 November 2005

Growing Up?

They who know!
And they who don't
It's part of growing up
Accepting what you have always known
The magic that is life!
Making the switch?
Is really a continuation
Teenager to adult!
How did you?

28 November 2005

The View?

All this music!
Puts me in the clouds
The music talks to me…
Puts me on the mountain
The view is breathtaking
Life is a blast!

28 November 2005

Going Home?

Going home?
Sixty-ish poems to go!
Show me the way
Please…
OK?
I will be fine doing the poems
It's…
The farmhouse!
Show me the way?
The poems?
Do what you like…
Just!
Let me go home…

28 November 2005

My Nan…

Picking brussels sprouts at six a.m.
All day in the shed…
Packing 'em
Three p.m. time to go!
We would meet outside work
Me? A five-year-old

Nan and her pushbike!
It had a kiddies' seat
I would meet her just for the lift
A full day!
I never heard her once complain
And again six a.m. tomorrow!
I didn't know then
But I know now…
God bless you!

29 November 2005

My Nan, Her Last Years

After Grandad had passed away
And I was in Corby
Nan was alone…
But then moved in with Mum and Dad
About the mid eighties
Nan's last couple of years…
She was in a wheelchair
Myself I was on a lot of medication
But still no excuse!
When Mum took Nan out (the town)
I had no time!
No time to push the wheelchair
I just wanted to get back to my music…
I just don't know what to say?
Nan gave me everything!
There isn't the words
Sorry!
I'm sorry…

29 November 2005

'Sorry'

My Nan, her last years!
Even now…
Would I have done it any different?

'Sorry'
Doesn't cover it!

29 November 2005

Tin Bath

Still with Nan and Grandad
Tin bath?
It was the very early sixties
A tin bath!
In front of the coal fire
How times have changed
A million memories
A million poems
Nan and Pop!
A million more memories
Mum…
But still?
A tin bath…

29 November 2005

If Not Now?

My vision…
Heaven on earth!
The heaven being within
Being happy
Being content
An end to poverty
(Bandwagon or not!)
The Third World
At home!
Everybody taking a step back
Look at yourself!
Slow down
Take the time to enjoy the magic
Talk to each other
Listen to each other

Communicate
Heaven on earth!
Heaven within
It's easy for me to say!
Sitting back
Feet up
On very good benefits
But still
What am I supposed to say?
This is the twenty-first century
If not now
When…?

29 November 2005

Put-down

Don, my Dad…
Always put me down
Sometimes you need that!
Or you would just fly and fly
The put-down!
Was it part of the big picture
Or was he just a crap father?
I remember…
I developed a sense of humour
To ease the atmosphere
Did he realise a young boy…
Could be that clever?
Thick!
Was his word
And still I hear him use it today…
Hey!
Who's thick?
Get it…

29 November 2005

Dad

I do love him…
He wants us to be best mates
Many a conversation!
But what is him?
And what is the drink?
Am I still thick?
When you're ten years old
You need a man
I don't need him so much now
Does he need me?
I love him!
But he can be difficult
I don't think I'll ever know
His real feelings
Which is a little sad
I do love him…

29 November 2005

One Flew over the Cuckoo's Nest

I always believed…
Being mentally ill was a game
Recently I've noticed it not
Some service users really are dim
A little time ago…
I heard Adam Ant saying…
'Hospital is not…
'*One Flew over the Cuckoo's Nest*
'There is no Jack Nicholson'
Fuck?
He really is Adam Ant!!!!
Look at the fun he could have had!
When I'm in
Everybody knows!!!!!!!
One Flew over the Cuckoo's Nest?
Come on!!!!!!!

30 November 2005

Advertising Space

Robbie on the radio!
His song…
'Advertising Space'
The King is dead!
Long live the King…
But hey?
When Jesus steps from the clouds
What deodorant?
What dog food?

1 December 2005

Give Peace a Chance?

Remember the sixties?
The hippies…
Love, love, love
I'm all for love!
I'm all for peace!
You should know that by now
But what if we didn't have soldiers?
What if we didn't defend?
Didn't make war?
Without
We may be without the freedom
To say…
John did say…
He didn't have the answers!
But still
You know the rest!

1 December 2005

War is Stupid!

War is not OK!
Terrorism is not OK!
My last poem…
Did not say otherwise!
When?
When will we learn?
War is stupid!
Killing is stupid!
When?

1 December 2005

Too Many Doors?

They who know!
And they who don't
We all knew once!
And still do…
You can lose it but!
Too many closed doors!
Too many put-downs…
They who know!
And they who don't
Come on!!!!!!!

1 December 2005

Everybody?

Maybe if I had accepted…
I had an illness
Accepted the drugs!
Didn't put up the fight
Maybe I would have got well
Much sooner
But what I saw in myself

I saw in everybody!
Illness?
What illness…?

2 December 2005

Recovery

My CPN
Just gave me the book…
In Recovery
But first!
I must accept I have an illness
What?
I hear you say!
I still don't know?!!!!!!!
It may not be important to you
But it is to me!
Define 'illness'
Is 'love' an illness?

2 December 2005

Teasing Me?

There she is!
The angel from heaven
Olney!
Is God a-teasing me?
Or what?
Eight-thirty p.m.
Loads of time!
An angel?
Oh yes…

2 December 2005

Washout?

What am I suppose to do?
I'm not a teenager!
Ten-thirty p.m.
Looks like tonight's a washout...

2 December 2005

Love Sucks?

At the dance tonight!
A young girl...
Her T-shirt said 'Love Sucks'
OK?
It was only a T-shirt!
Yes, may be love sucks!
But when you understand a little
It's the ups and downs
That make it happen
Makes the magic!
Enjoy the ride...

2 December 2005

In Vain

If you suffer from positive paranoia
Or just paranoia...
And you believe someone's watching!
It may well be...
The born-again Christian thing!
And in fact it's God that's watching.
To fall short of God
You have to accept that there is a God!
And maybe your paranoia being Him.
If you have these feelings
Take the time to sort it out...

You're a long time dead!
Heaven or hell?
God watching!
Is a state of mind
Which can be switched at any time!
By anything…
But difficult to lose

3 December 2005

Good by Bad?

If you suffer from negative paranoia
Everybody's out to get you!
Bad thoughts and ideas
This may be the 'Devil' at work?
Myself, I don't believe in demons…
But if you do
Again sort it out!
When I experience something bad
Yes it's bad!
But is it trying to show me the good
By being bad…?
Heaven and hell?
Sort it out…

3 December 2005

Embrace It!

Life?
Life is to be embraced!
Good or bad?
Turn it around
You only get the one shot!
Life is not a rehearsal
Don't wish your life away…
Yesterday never again!
Enjoy the ride!
If it's not working?

Sort it out!
Life?
Embrace it!

3 December 2005

Dean Within

Jimmy Dean…
Looking for answers
Not letting anyone in?
All the time
That's where it was
Within
You know your questions…
And yes your answers!
Jimmy Dean I'm not
Jimmy Dean?
That's your lot!

4 December 2005

Big Big Star!

Showaddywaddy!
David Essex…
The album *Step Two*
Gonna Make You a Star!
Forty-five years old!
Still dreaming…
Big, big star!
When do you stop
Stop dreaming…?

4 December 2005

Fame or Freedom?

When my book gets published
Will I lose my freedom?

Should I hold back?
It's not like I have a deal
The dotted line…
But if I did…
Fame or freedom?
The poems are yours!

4 December 2005

Where Are You?

End of part nine!
Forty poems to go…
Is no one going to find me?
Exploit me…
Hanging on the telephone!
Where are you?

4 December 2005

II.x

It's Not the End, 2005

Bug?

I know a man, a friend
Who believes that he is bugged!
A microchip in his head.
Well? Years back, in hospital
When I was in
They always showed this film on the TV
Gregory Peck, maybe?
Anyhow…
It was about the Russians and Americans
A spy thriller!
With the British guy bugged (in his head).
Life can be quite bizarre
We try to put answers to it…
My friend may have many coincidences happening?
He's not stupid!
Medication can and does do all sorts to the mind.
Personally I believe…
It's part of the bigger picture
Making people paranoid, God-fearing!
Or is that my paranoia?
You know the rest…

5 December 2005

Low Esteem

Out on the town!
Saturday night…

Young men and women
Drunk, out of it!
At the foot of the mountain
What's the point?
It's all been done…
Nothing's new?
If only they knew…
In time,
The magic!
Right now?
'Give us another drink…'

5 December 2005

Home-made!

Many have travelled the world
Looking for answers
India and
All around…
Myself?
I have never left home
My poems…
Are all home-made
England!
In my head
One day…
I would like to see the world
Maybe?

5 December 2005

Medication

Modecate injections with
Kemadrin for side-effects
Natalie conceived and born
Depixol injections again
Kemadrin…
Luke conceived and born

Loads of nicotine
A few spliffs
Very little alcohol
2005...
Olanzapine 5mg
Nocturnal
A few other meds
These being the main

5 December 2005

It's Over?

All my life!
I have been walking...
Walking up this hill
It's over!
I'm walking down...
Down the other side
I have explained myself
I've found God!
I can sleep with peace
One last thing?
Passing it on...
Finding a publisher
If you're reading this?
Finally...
It's over?

6 December 2005

Wank!

It's not the end of the world!
Take your finger off the button
And have a wank!
'Release the pressure'

6 December 2005

Stuart Adamson

Thank you! Stuart Adamson
Big Country
1993 my divorce!
Your song 'Ships'
1993 you came to Corby!
I was in the hospital
Loads of medication, but made the gig…
Your song 'Alone'
With the medication kicking in
My age?
My music!
All the shit went from my head!
No more racing thoughts
Still to this day…
My head is clear
Sometimes I have to put a thought there
It's that clear!
The power of music!
God bless you…
Stuart Adamson RIP

6 December 2005

Paradox

A writer writes a song
The song has meaning and appeal
The writer makes lots of money
The paradox
Is it creative and art?
Or is it the money?
Paradox?
If I become a millionaire…
Does that kill my poems?

8 December 2005

Lost and Found?

Did I find God?
Or did God find me?
Define 'God'

8 December 2005

Live For Ever!

Rockabilly bop!
1981
American fifties Rockabilly
The birth of British Rockabilly…
Psychobilly!
Stevenage to London
Rock bop!
New Romantics
Out the way!
1981
Live for ever!
Rockabilly bop
A-do bop…

8 December 2005

Do It All Again!

Rockabilly bop a-do bop!
2005
The Charlotte…
DONS
Drapes of Northampton Society
The British Railway
Kick-ass psychobilly!
From Europe
Tiger Army LA
Do it all again…

Forty-five
Today!

8 December 2005

Sixes and Sevens

All being well…
I should be finished me poems
This month!
2006…
I'll be looking for a publisher
The deal
All being well?
Published in 2007
But not '06
Why?
Six is the number of the demons
Seven the number for God!
OK?
I'm not 'God'
But I also ain't a demon!
Sixes and sevens

11 December 2005

Dove

The new Pope, 2005
In the window
On the TV!
Set free a white dove
A symbol of freedom
Peace…
The dove flew back!
Right back in the window
Behind him
So…
To be free?
You have to want to be free

Ask yourself…
Are we ready?

11 December 2005

Love Poison

Once it starts!
You can't stop…
Take your time?
Find the right one
Oh yes!
Love is the drug
Release the pressure?
Love poison
Let it out…
Those temples
Ease the load
It ain't a sin
What is a sin!
Unwanted love…
Love poison!
Get it?

11 December 2005

Stepping on Toes

People say to me…
Why not work in Africa?
Why not be an advocate…
For people with mental health problems?
My reply…
'There are millions of people
'We all have to find a place
'In the jigsaw.
'Me? I've got my poems…
'Why step on another's toes?'

11 December 2005

Sitting on the Fence?

I suppose…
I'm sitting on the fence
Christian life?
Worldly life…
OK!
I'm going for the worldly life…
But in that life
I believe
I can give others a leg-up
Maybe?
A Christian?
In a worldly life
Yes OK!
I know…
Sitting on the fence?

11 December 2005

Prejudice…

Paranoia and God?
You all know my poems
But ask yourself
Why are you paranoid?
Coincidences happen!
Things happen…
We're all paranoid
To a degree
Stop!
For a moment
Love is in the air!
Is it Jesus?
Is it God?
Don't let your prejudice…
Always win?

11 December 2005

Live and Let Live

Jesus Christ!
Calvary Hill…
John Lennon!
New York…
Will we never learn?
Live and let live…
Myself…
An old man maybe?

12 December 2005

Misunderstood?

There will be some
Who still don't get it?
Metaphors?
Sometimes it's the only way to say
The message I'm giving
I cannot make any simpler
'The Bible'
It's about making the connection
I hope I have helped
It is in all of us…

12 December 2005

Facing Your Demons?

If you have demons
Something in your childhood maybe?
Yes! Oh Yes!
I'm all for sorting it out!
Facing your demons!
But first be sure…
Be sure you're ready?
Demons, devils and monsters…
Can take you by surprise

Just because you're an adult
Don't mean a thing
Demons, devils and monsters?
Sort it out!
But be sure you're ready?
Facing your demons!

12 December 2005

Starry Stars

Stars in the night sky
Guiding sailors across the seas
Shore to shore
Stars in the night
I need you once more
Guide me home
Bring me in
Take me under your wing
Don't let me down now?
Stars in the night sky
You have got me this far
Shine once more
Starry stars
In the night sky
Thank you one and all!

12 December 2005

In the Clouds

Sitting in school…
Looking out the window
Watching the clouds roll by…
Apart from the chalk duster flying through the air
The clouds were far more interesting
I was good at:
        Art
        Woodwork
        Tech drawing

Left school, couldn't read and write
I remember
I always wanted to be good…
Maths and English
Head in the clouds
I guess?

12 December 2005

What Will Be?

Two thousand years ago
Jesus standing on a hill
Today, TV books music
General education…
Another thousand years?
We will still be talking…
The same old same
What will be
The new…?

12 December 2005

It's Not the End!

The world will spin
The sun will shine
For at least a very long time…
For as long as there's a human
There will be a heaven
In the idea of his mind!
Even without my poems
Because if not my poems
Another's
The world will spin
The sun will shine
It's not the end!
And very likely never was?

15 December 2005

You and Me!

Earthquakes…
Hurricanes…
Tidal waves…
Take care of your home!
Our home!
Mother Earth…
Earthquakes
Hurricanes
Tidal waves
You have been warned!
We have been warned!
The wind is blowing…
Don't leave it to them…
Don't leave it to they?
It's you and me!
Earthquakes
Hurricanes
Tidal waves…

15 December 2005

Catch a Rainbow?

A pot of gold?
A pocket full of dreams…
The rainbow will move…
The closer you get!
One day?
Just maybe…
It will all happen
Read my words…
Make it happen?
Catch that rainbow…
Then set it free…
For you and me!

16 December 2005

Destiny?

Writing this poem
Is it my 'destiny' to write this poem?
If I hadn't written it
Would that also have been my destiny?
Not writing it!
Get it?
Do we make our own destiny?
I believe we don't!
Are my poems going to be a bestseller?
That's not down to me…
Destiny?
Tomorrow?
Who knows…

16 December 2005

You Looking at Me?

What you looking at?
You looking at me?
Remember!
It works both ways
I'm looking at you!
With love…

16 December 2005

All I Ever Wanted…

All I ever wanted…
Was and still is
To love!
And to be loved
Forty-five years young!
It ain't over yet

Do I believe?
I believe…

17 December 2005

Am I God?

You have read my poems!
Do I think I am God?
Am I making myself a God?
What are you asking?
Define 'God'
You have read my poems…
No!
Definitely No!
A god I am not…

17 December 2005

Am I Jesus?

You have read my poems!
Do I think I am Jesus?
Am I making myself the second coming?
To a degree, yes!
In a logical way, but no more than anyone other
'Jesus' is in all of us
You have read my poems…
You tell me?
Until then?
Keep watching the skies

17 December 2005

Where Are You?

'DAD?'
Where are you?
What are you waiting for?

You know who you are!
Come and say hello…
All I want
Is to see those eyes!

18 December 2005

Bullet in a Bible

First World War
Second World War
Any war…
Bullet in a Bible
Top pocket?
Saved his life…
Eight-hundred poems
Eight-hundred bullets
How many lives?
Make the connection
Live for ever
Through…
Jesus Christ! Amen.

18 December 2005

Stardust?

The earth does not belong to us
We belong to it!
Like a rose in the garden
A tree in the breeze
We grew from the earth
And in dust we shall return
The Big Bang?
Stardust we are…

18 December 2005

CCTV

I'm all for CCTV
If you don't do wrong
It's in your favour
And catches the bad ones, right?
Last night!
Thirty-five mph
Speed camera
The streets were empty
£60 fine
Three penalty points
It's not my first!
That's
CCTV!

18 December 2005

Promise Fulfilled

Letchworth Garden City…
Town Centre 1979
My world falling apart!
Hand over my eyes…
Made an unspoken promise
Be careful what you promise!
My book is now in your hands
If you are that girl?
Promise fulfilled!
Love always…

18 December 2005

Far-cure

1982
Bedford South-wing
Breaking up words again…

'Colin Farquhar'
Calling Far-cure
A plaster for the world?

21 December 2005

How Was It For You?

Different drugs…
i.e. different medications
Give you different realities
I remember one time…
I could feel the earth move!
How was it for you?

21 December 2005

It's Not the End…

This is my last poem…
In my two books
Tomorrow, Today
But!
It's not the end of my poetry
We all could write a million 'love' poems
But I want to fall in love
And experience them as I write them
It's not the end…

21 December 2005

III

III.i

End of Book Two, 2006

A State of Mind?

Take all of your tomorrows
Take all of your yesterdays
Bring them together
For the moment
And you have all the time in the world
A state of mind…
Tomorrow is not important
Yesterday the same!

1 January 2006

A Tear…

Watching the U2 DVD…
Vertigo – Live from Chicago
My book?
It ain't over yet
A tear…

2 January 2006

Cock and Fanny!

Cock and Fanny!
That's it
There is nothing else
But also…
The perception
Knowing what this means?

Love?
So many lie…

7 January 2006

Baby Blue

I've got a girl
Her name…
'Baby Blue'
She knows how to party!
Oh yes…
Am I wise to her?
I hope so
You see…
She's had some lovers
My old pal,
Gene
He was the one…
Who put me wise!
He's dead
But she won't have me
'Baby Blue'

8 January 2006

The Poem?

Writing the poem…
Isn't the problem
The problem comes
In another reading it…

8 January 2006

Yobs…

Yobs…
Trouble-makers

Antisocial behaviour
Stick some fucking drugs in 'em
The shit I've been through
I never did anyone any harm
Drugs!
Believe me
That would sort 'em out
Some of the old meds!

10 January 2006

Vision?

'Vision'
Sometimes…
It's just seeing what's in front of you!
Do you?

12 January 2006

All-consuming

I have an illness
I don't recognise
What if it is so…
All-consuming
I can't see the wood
For the trees?

14 January 2006

English

There is something…
In the English language
Only the English…
Get!
You can learn 'English'
ABC

But if you ain't…
English?

15 January 2006

Flying Colours

Music?
My music collection…
The Exam
Flying colours

15 January 2006

Every Word!

Bullshit!
What do I know?
I'm mentally ill…
Bullshit?
Every word…

15 January 2006

Interesting?

The Government
Likely have a file on you
Ask yourself…
Are you interesting?

15 January 2006

Safety in Numbers

It doesn't work…
If my book only sells
A couple of hundred

The few would say…
Who's this nutter?

15 January 2006

Badness?

Why is there so much…
Badness in the world?
It's a miff!
There really is bucketloads of good…
The bad is misunderstood
He's trying to inspire you to be good

15 January 2006

Timeless

Pop music
As a time and place
By its very nature
Rockin' music
Is and always will be timeless…

15 January 2006

Secret Club

Perception?
What side are you?
'Secret club'
Freedom?
Freedom takes grace and money
Perception gives you freedom
But without some money…
Perception…
What side are you?

16 January 2006

Get Well Soon!

Twenty-five years…
They don't want you well!
'Get well soon'
A joke…
Are you in on the joke?
Get well soon,
Not!

16 January 2006

No More Games…

Everybody knows!
Strangers…
Friends…
The new guy?
Expectations…
All eyes on you!
Fed up!
Had enough
No more games…
It's not down to you!
Everybody knows…
Everybody knows
It's you!

16 January 2006

Kiss the Sky!

Raindrops…
Falling from the sky
Tears…
A thousand angels
The angels
Weep for you!

What are you to do?
But
Kiss the sky!
This night…

16 January 2006

No More Promises

Promises?
I've had promises up to the back teeth
Promises?
I'm all out of promises
Promises?
No more promises for me to keep

16 January 2006

The Human Race

God?
There is no God!
God!
God is the human race…
What can another do for you?
A real person!
God?
In heaven
God…
Is the human race!
God…
So called?
God!
It's all bollocks

16 January 2006

Jesus is a Fool

Jesus nailed to the cross!
His Dad didn't help him…
Jesus believed
Jesus was a fool…
I'm a fool!
My father, don't give a toss
I'm alone
Alone on this cross
A fool…
With no one to love
Jesus is a fool
Aren't we all?

16 January 2006

Believe?

I believe in 'Good and Bad'
I believe in 'Love'
I believe in 'The Wind and the Rain'
I believe in 'Music'
I believe in 'Song Lyrics'
I believe in 'Money'
I believe in 'Friendship'
Do I believe in 'God'?
Do I believe that there is a 'God'?
I believe in 'The Human Race'
'Real People'
If that is 'God'? Then yes!
God in heaven?
God who made Creation?
I believe in the 'God' in my mind!
And how it all works
And how it all fits into place
What about the Church and the Bible?
I don't understand my daughter's blind faith and devotion
Then she seems to be afraid or offended by my poems

I believe in believing
Rather than not believing…

16 January 2006

Formula

Once you understand…
The formula
Song lyrics…
Me poems…
It's easy to write
But harder to be stimulated by

17 January 2006

Who But the Bad?

Who wants my book?
Who wants my poems?
My dreams…
Not the good!
They don't need inspiring
They're already good!
The Devil or the bad…
That's who!
Sorry my dreams ain't for sale
My dreams?
Who?
Who but the bad…

17 January 2006

Set Me Free…

How long?
How long do you want me on this cross?
Take me down!
Set me free…

Save yourself…
I only have some words
You have to feel it…
Only you!
Only you know, you
Let it be?
Set me free…

17 January 2006

This Rubbish?

Why do I write such rubbish?
Imagination!
When you ain't getting any love…
Your imagination runs wild!
Jesus?
A virgin maybe…
That guy!
Had imagination

17 January 2006

Midwinter Blues

Everywhere I go…
Everybody seems to know
Me and my ideas…
How?
Apart from pop music
But that could be singing about anyone
I just feel like giving up
But I have nothing to give up
Do I?

17 January 2006

The Dream…

My ideas…
My poems…
Am I killing the dream?
Am I fulfilling the dream?
The mystery…
The dream…

17 January 2006

Size?

Size?
Does size matter?
Big!
Is OK for sex
Quality!
For making babies
Big?
Just misses the target

17 January 2006

Conviction

My daughter!
Do I understand?
It's about conviction…
Following the one!
Football team
Pop star!
But not listening to others
Surely is a root for trouble…
Whether she's right or wrong?
She has…
Conviction!

18 January 2006

Taboo

When I talk of...
'Jesus' and sometimes 'the Bible'
I am using it as a reference
To describe my feelings
If we did not have the Bible
I would still be having these feelings
And writing about them
We all have these feelings...
But it may be taboo
To talk about it...

18 January 2006

Psyche

'God' didn't help Jesus...
Because there is no God!
God is the human race!
And how it all fits together
'Jesus' created heaven...
Heaven in the human psyche
Believe in 'Jesus'!!!!!
Or at least the idea
Jesus is the key...

18 January 2006

All of Us!

One person?
One person does not make heaven!
'Jesus' needs us!
As much as we need him
Believing?

18 January 2006

Influences

My real father don't give a toss!
Don my Dad only put me down…
So who is my Dad?
You!
'The human race'
Every conversation I've ever heard
Pop songs, TV
Rock and roll…
My influences?
Everything…
At least Jesus didn't have the TV
But still…
Every fucker…
Put the boot in
Get it?

18 January 2006

Preacher?

I'm not a preacher!
I just have a few ideas
Of course I'd like to be successful
A writer…
A preacher?
I'm not!

19 January 2006

Play the Game…

OK?
So I won't be famous
In my lifetime…
You know!

I know!
Play the game…

19 January 2006

Go to Sleep…

Hey?
What's the problem…
Why all these poems?
Stop!
Slow down…
It's not important!
Tomorrow?
Another day…
Go to sleep…
You done this to me!
Your stupid pills
Go to sleep?
Let go…

19 January 2006

I Wish?

They tell me…
God doesn't deal in money
OK?
It's not a prayer
It's a wish
The Lotto

19 January 2006

III.ii

Flogging a Dead Horse, 2006

No More Deadlines...

I'm free!
No more deadlines...
Free...
Free to fall in love
Kiss the sky!
Mountains?
A problem not
Free...

16 March 2006

Solitary Confinement

I have so much...
I'm free!
With the grace
To know this
The world is full of lonely people
My phone has not rung for a week...
My friend?
My music...
Do I have to live forever
In dreams...?
What about those?
Without a dream...
Lonely?
You can only take so much...

Then what?
Lonely…
And take it again…
If you feel this poem
Tell me your answer…
If you don't?
Pray you never do…
Lonely…

16 March 2006

Lover Please…

Too many
Different lovers
And you're on that road.
You may be looking for something
Which doesn't exist
Or you had it all the time, but didn't notice.
Rocky road blues
Heartbreak hotel
Bottle of pills…
The dice are thrown
The cards are dealt
If only it were that simple.
Lover please…
Please come back.

16 March 2006

Tell Him…

They do say…
'It's your dreams that make you who you are'
Well…
I'm walking around the other side
No more horizons
I'm there…
But still?
The dream is not complete

Tell me…
What did I do wrong?

17 March 2006

Not Just William

William and his Mum…
Walking through town
William stops
He wants his Mum to look at something!
She just keeps walking…
The abuse from William vocals!
'WANK HEAD, wanker…'
His Mum is a single parent
With a physical disability
A bad foot…
Anyhow?
William then starts to push and pull…
Some shopping hits the ground
In hindsight I wished I'd said something
But then, maybe not?
The mother has let her boy down…
Big time
No respect and little love
The boy is eight or nine?
It shouldn't have been left to get this far
You can see it in his eyes…

18 March 2006

Magic People…

The magic people
Have all gone away
Today!
Maybe it's the cold?
I was not told
Magic people
I wish they would stay

Three years!
Time to find another's game
I wish?
Magic people…
You know!
Come again
One day…

21 March 2006

Never to Be…

Night after night…
On my own!
Weeks' years
Slowly disappear
I'm scared to say 'boo'
Waiting for the dream!
Even if?
I would still be a prisoner
To the idea
The idea that is me?
Scared to crack the egg!
There is no egg
Night after night…
In this dream
There is no dream!
Just an idea
That will never be!
Because if it was?
Then it would not…

27 March 2006

I Wish I Didn't Know…

I wish I didn't know
What I know now!
Which is…
'It's not important

'It doesn't matter'
'Coz before
I had a goal
Which was…
Finding out!
It's not important
It doesn't matter…

1 April 2006

Knock on Wood

We're all sitting here
So pretty…
Listening to the music
A drunk…
Dancing next to the speaker
Alone!
OK?
He's had it hard
A few knocks
Is he free?
Free in his depression
Maybe?
Are we free?
We've all had the knocks
We can't all dance next to the speaker
Can we?

1 April 2006

Self-destruct

Thirty to forty
Years old…
We all have the dream…
The perfect relationship
The reality?
The self-destruct button

Before we get anywhere near a relationship
We hit the button…

1 April 2006

Who's Ill?

When you're manic
You may talk of 'Jesus'
When actually it's the enlightenment
And the need to pass it on!
When you're manic…
Everything is larger than life
The enlightenment…
We all have
Even the so-called normal
Different people different ways…
The manic are suppressed with many different drugs
That's why when it takes off
It's even more so…!
'The enlightenment…'

2 April 2006

What Is It?

Enlightenment…
What is it?
Communication…
Feelings…
How it all works!
Which can be a sensation…
Feelings!
Words…
Music…
More than two or three words anywhere
Communication!
A story…
A film…

Life…
Being alive…
Love…
Hey!
Love…
Enlightenment…
Get it?

2 April 2006

True…

True enlightenment
Is when you let go…
Eight-hundred and fifty poems
Why?
Time to let go…

2 April 2006

Lay Them Down…

We all know…
How complicated politics can be
But!
What if
Everybody
With a killing machine
Laid them down?
No more killing!
No more war!
Some…
Only know war
Because of a war somewhere
I have the freedom of speech
But hey
Come on…
Lay them down…
I kid no one

Do I?
Why?

2 April 2006

High?

The greatest high?
Is being normal…
Forget the drugs!
Alcohol…
But!
To taste the sweet
You have to try the bad
Maybe…

3 April 2006

Alive…

Lying here in my bed
Writing this poem
My heart is beating
I am breathing
Why?
How?
I'm alive
Alive?
What is alive?
OK!
I'm not dead
Come on!
Alive…
What is alive?
You may have a simple answer
Think again?
Alive…
Alive and kicking…

3 April 2006

Nowhere to Go…

The Bungalow…
The Mental Health System
I feel have let me down
For years I have been suppressed with medication
Which in turn
Has given me the insight to do my poems
But!
At the end of the day…
I haven't written anything anybody didn't know anyway
I'm forty-six next month
I've been on my own for years
Where's my family?
My possible family…
Swallowed up with medication
Pills and shit!
I sometimes feel…
The whole world is playing a game with me
I can't let go…
Because there's nowhere to go

5 April 2006

Ticket…

My book
These poems
My desire
My ticket…
Which is?
My illness

10 April 2006

Why?

Twenty whatever years ago
I was set on fire

The fire still burns
With desire…
The desire to explain
The desire

10 April 2006

Not So Crazy

Tuesday the 11th
April 2006
First time ever…
My mother said out loud
'You're not so crazy'
Fuck?
How long have I waited
How long?

11 April 2006

Get a Life?

Why do I think
It's me…?
I'm not intelligent
Far better books out there…
Me?
To bring the world together
Schizophrenia
That's what it is
Forget 'Jesus'
Move on…
Get a life?
This is my life…

11 April 2006

Around the Corner?

Just got my reply
Forward press, Peterborough
Sorry!
No joy…
That's it
I don't know anybody else
But!
Who knows
What's around the corner?
I ain't dead yet…

12 April 2006

My Crossroads

Sitting here thinking
Just thinking…
Not a lot to think about
Sitting here
Looking down the road
Just closed doors
My crossroads
Four dead-end signs
The sun is shining…
What do I need with doors?
What do I need with roads?
I am me
I'm alive
My crossroads
Me!

12 April 2006

My Crossroads

Written

Do I need a publisher…?
Do I need a big movie…?
Just the fact it's written
It's me…
My life…
Every day I wake up…
I'm the big star in my own life
Any auditions…
The leading lady?

12 April 2006

Written #2

On a more serious note
I have always believed…
That some of my ideas are important
But again
The fact that it is written
Should be enough
Published or not…

12 April 2006

Mixed Up

The early eighties
When I first tried putting some words together
I couldn't spell at all…
Loads of medication…
Very mixed up!
But I remember I had this need
Something inside…
Most went straight in the bin

I even burned some
I remember I had this one called 'Sleep Walk'
It was about walking through different generations in time...
Did anyone go in the bins?
A couple of years later
Highlander was a big hit...
No way could I have done the story in the film...
But I sincerely believe some of my ideas have kicked-started other ideas
Hey I'm mental...
Mixed up
I can say anything!
I'm not even published...

12 April 2006

One

I believe
Me and my life
Have inspired
Many a song
Pop or not.
What happens
When the world becomes 'one'?
We're in each other's pocket now.
Get a life
Not mine
Or me yours

12 April 2006

What's Reality?

Paranoia...
The TV and the radio
Have told me...
That they are making a movie
With me...
The leading role

It's in the making
Right now!
Now I've written it down
It's sounds daft
Reality?
What's reality
Is it the pills…
Is it me?

16 April 2006

That Horse?

Why?
Why am I still writing?
Haven't I said enough?
How much rope do they need?
I've said all I can…
Flogging a dead horse

16 April 06

Life and Soul of the Party

What's the point
Being…
The life and soul of the party?
That's me!
With…
Just four walls

17 April 2006

Interrupted

I've been on my own for so long –
Busy doing nothing –
That when something does happen

I'm interrupted
I want to get back to doing nothing
Nothing!
Just nothing…

17 April 2006

State of Mind

Busy doing nothing
Is a state of mind
Yes I'm doing nothing
But I feel things
Everything…

17 April 2006

Two Steps Ahead

Pop stars
Middle-aged pop stars
Looking for their crown?
Forget it boys!
I'm two steps ahead
Every album
Pushes me forward…

17 April 2006

In the Dip

Feeling down…
Not a lot happening
My roller coaster
In the dip

17 April 2006

Pop Music (The Idea)

Take a look at your own music collection; what are you listening to? Even the radio – some, most are simple boy/girl love songs…

Usually there's a line or a word that changes all that. In my opinion there is no such thing as a simple pop song! The writers are constantly looking to change your perception, move things along. Why? Where does it all end?

Pop music itself can be an education…

The Idea?

I believe pop music is singing to an idea…

A progression to bring about 'the second coming'.

But, in this, 'the second coming' is not one person; it is the education of enlightenment and the changing of one's perception.

Controlled medication, the misuse of drugs and alcohol are all part of the above!

How many times have you said to a friend: Listen? But they don't hear it, or they choose not to hear it? Sometimes even with friends it can be taboo to talk about music…

Do they have pop music in Bethlehem?

17 April 2006

Regardless

No matter how high
No matter how low
Sunshine
Rain clouds
Manic or well
The world keeps a-turning…

21 April 2006

Love?

You don't have to be in love
To be in love
Sometimes you understand more
Looking from a far
Myself…
I am Mr Love
But
I don't even know how to say 'hi' to a female
I have so many feelings…
Love?

21 April 2006

Following It?

All this enlightenment
I keep talking about…
Once you get it
Do you follow it?
It's hard not to…
Either you're bad, really quite bad
Or you never got it?
When you've seen the light
Everything becomes so simple
And the bad pointless
It's not about words!
It's something inside
Only you know…
No one can tell you

21 April 2006

The Truth

The truth…
The truth is so simple

So many choose not to see it
The truth
We all step over it
The truth?
Can be a lie…
But the truth
Is the truth
Today!
Always…

21 April 2006

III.iii

The Disease, Spring 2006

No Way Back!

It's gone too far this time!
I know who I am…
The magic people
Have shown me their magic
Narnia
Isn't just a story
It's you and me
In the wardrobe of our mind
Yes it's all quiet…
No way back!
No way back to not knowing
Tell me when you're ready…
No way back…

23 April 2006

The Disease

Mac me old buddy
Gave us the song…
'The Disease'
On the album *Heaven Up Here*
We all know it's not his disease
Jesus on Calvary said
'It is done'
Jesus put the virus
In the computer

23 April 2006

Understanding

Understanding your illness
Must be a big part in its cure
Schizophrenia…
Bipolar?
In my experience
No one is willing to tell you anything
My illness
Is my desire
Triggered by the mystery that is lovemaking
These days…
I don't really know
Drug addiction maybe?

23 April 2006

Untitled

My poems…
My desire to make it in the world
But more importantly
The content of my poems
That's my illness.
When
And if…
I will be cured
Then what I'm famous for
Will be no more…

23 April 2006

Inspiration or Answer?

When you listen…
To a song
Do you
Take that as the answer?

i.e.
'Let It Be', Paul McCartney.
Or do you
Take it as inspiration?

23 April 2006

Different?

Sorry!
If I repeat myself
But!
I do try to make each poem different

24 April 2006

Fairytales

Do you believe…
Fairytales?
It's not about the story
It's the magic
I believe…
Yes!

24 April 2006

Sin?

A sin is only a sin
If you know you are sinning
If you sin in innocence
Like when you're a child
It is not a sin
It's not just the Ten Commandments
We all know when…
You just know…

24 April 2006

Sin #2

Can you sin
If you don't believe in God?
More so!
You are sinning to the sin
If you don't believe?
Ask…
Your broken heart

24 April 2006

The Penny Drops!

I always believed…
My 'nervous breakdowns' were special
Sent from 'heaven…'
Twenty whatever years later
The penny drops!
It's so obvious
Somebody put something in my drink
Do you know what it's like to trip
When you don't know you're tripping…?
Then the shit in hospital…
More drugs!
All these years and what for?
Nothing…
The joke?
I believe everybody knew all along…
Sad…
I feel so sad
You don't know?

26 April 2006

Sick of It…

Every waking moment
My mind revolves around this delusion

My illness…
I'm truly fed up
Sick of it!
I wish I were somebody else
If it were real
If I were somebody
Then maybe?
Sick of it!
Just sick of it
Sad and lonely…

26 April 2006

Alice in Wonderland?

Jesus was chosen…
The people around him helped him along the way
If we believe the Bible
Jesus himself believed it
In my life and experiences
People are trying to make me into something
The difference being
I can see it!
Nine-hundred poems I believe in, yes!
But are drugs reality?
Jesus I'm not!
Alice in Wonderland?
Maybe…

26 April 2006

Dues!

I have no more
What do you want from me?
I do not live in a fantasy!
Secretly you know this
Dues!
Pay me my dues
Let me go home…

28 April 2006

Sanity Check

Mental health…
Touches one in three
Yes we are all different!
Different experiences…
Some?
Must be on a similar trip to me
My book!
These poems…
A sanity check maybe?
Feedback!
Shine a light for me
I also need…

28 April 2006

Voices

I don't hear voices
I have never heard voices
Only real voices…
Like the TV
And in my music
Of course other people!
In my head…
My thoughts
My ideas
Maybe mixed up with the above
But!
I don't hear voices
And never have

30 April 2006

Singing You or Me?

When a singer writes a song
And it seems like he's singing about you

Forget it!
He's singing about himself
They just change…
The you and me bit
Etc…

30 April 2006

Voices #2

Do you understand?
The voices
TV, music, etc…
The TV and music
Have an audience of millions
Some bits
Are bound to hit home!
And if you're paranoid
More bits…

30 April 2006

I Bet that You Look a Prat on the Dance Floor

Because I'm…
Suppressed with medication
Anywhere near a dance floor
I take off!

30 April 2006

Too Many Neighbours…

Drove around…
Looked across!
They have killed it…
The dream is dead!
A whole housing estate and more
Legoland…

The farmhouse
In fantastic stone
Sticks out like a sore thumb
Dead!
The dream is dead
Too many neighbours…

30 April 2006

I'm Done…

Elated for three years!
Drugs? Whatever…
The wind has gone from my sails
A little deflated!
No more 'farmhouse'
Giving up the Lotto maybe
Me poems?
Well I'm writing this one
Is this all part of the plan?
They haven't told me
Until the next time…
I'm done!

30 April 2006

Demon Year?

2006
Is this my demon year?
Waiting for 2007
I don't have demons
Race with the Devil?
I don't have a Hot-rod
Be-Bop-a-Lula

30 April 2006

This Is It?

All my life
I've dreamt of being well-off
Spot the Ball…
The Lotto
This is it
Maybe?
Chillout!
Accept what you've got
Waiting for the promises of tomorrow?
Tomorrow you'll be in your box
Today!
It's today
This is it
Live it…

30 April 2006

Fuck the Ozone!

Gas up and go!
Fuck the ozone…
Shag the Mother
Not!

30 April 2006

Let Sleeping Dogs Lie

If this book?
My poems
Are my fire!
Why set anyone else alight?

1 May 2006

Snow White

My daughter constantly looks down on my poetry
Me and my ideas!
She hardly phones
And never visits…
Why?
Because of her new and much better family
The Church!

1 May 2006

When All's Well!

Opening new doors…
Forty-six years old!
When will I put it behind me?
When will I be well?
The day I don't need to write a poem
Maybe?

3 May 2006

Signs

Looking for the signs…
Everything has its time and place!
My poems…
Will they ever see the light of day?
Destiny?
I believe in destiny

3 May 2006

First Day of My Life…

I've been a-reading
Me poems…

I never read my poems!
End of 2003
A big change!
Negative to positive
The same subject
'The Dream'
But I never said what the dream was –
The dream of being alive!
In love
Your first love…
The birds a-singing!
The wind in your hair
Rock 'n' roll
The day I crossed the line
Perception!
Saw the world how I saw it
Suppressed
Medication
They took my life…
Forty-six years old…
What now?
I ain't dead yet!

4 May 2006

Crossing the Line?

You may have read about it?
You may be with friends?
You may have a close family?
You may never experience it?
You may have always have been there?
The day you cross the line!
Drug-induced, I don't know?
Perception…
Seeing the world for the first time!
On your own!
1979
You don't know anything about it
The rest of your life!
Trying to tell everybody

Still nobody says a word…
You were never crazy!
But, all my life to find this out
The bastards!

4 May 2006

On Ice

The 1970s, maybe 1980
I said about the new Bible
The soldiers were on the move
A new breed of pop star
The needles and shit were ready
On ice
I was put on ice
Writing my book…

5 May 2006

Within

Looking through my poems
I didn't realise
Now many depressing ones I'd written
I remember…
Even at my most depressed
I always had this love within
Always…

5 May 2006

Destiny?

I believe in destiny!
Yes!
But what if it's my destiny
To work in a factory?
Big wheel

Little wheel…?
Destiny?

5 May 2006

Love, Just Love

When I was a young man
On my motorbike
Driving home from college
Or on a night out…
I would see the towns from the countryside
Lit up like Christmas trees
It always made me feel lonely
These days that's all spun around
And I get great comfort from the lights
It sounds daft…
But love, I feel love from the towns
When I was a boy
I was always looking; I just wanted to fit in somewhere
Now?
I fit in with myself
And the love in the space around me…
Spiritual maybe?
Love, just love

5 May 2006

Get Out of Jail

Giving up the weed…
Smoking a fag every twenty minutes?
Turn the key…
Get out of prison
Giving up the weed…
Is to be set free!

5 May 2006

The Fix

Gave up the nicotine
January 2003
Gave up the needle
May 2003
The needle once a fortnight
My meds!
It wasn't just about the meds
It was the fix
Sometimes the pain
My whole world would be in fortnights
Working out the Kemadin
My moods?
The moods caused by the medicine
Not my illness
Giving anything up…
Is about timing, finding the right time
May 2006
Is it time to put it all behind me?
The meds may help you…
Believe me they're also the problem
The fix!
Time to move on?

5 May 2006

Different Worlds!

BBC six o'clock news
Tonight!
Paranoid schizophrenic
Murders pregnant woman…!
What the fuck?
I'm a paranoid schizophrenic…
My illness is meant to be – read my book
I wouldn't tread on an ant
Even at my worst, my very worst
It's all a laugh…

Different worlds!
Kill the bastard?
The damage is done…

5 May 2006

Are You Happy?

Some of my poems…
I may sound bitter?
Hey!
I'm not bitter
I've got a great life
I wouldn't change anything!
My world is an adventure
The next U2 album is just for me…
The Bunnymen, 2nd of June
I wouldn't be anybody else!
Happy?
It's all a laugh

5 May 2006

Ungrateful?

A lifetime of medication
So many questions…
At times I can be so ungrateful
It's not just words and ideas that get mixed up
Your whole nervous system can be on fire
The thing that always bugged me, big time, is:
They never talked it over
In went the needles
Which poses the question, how much of it is drug addiction?
Times have changed I believe…
But that's only from my point of view
What if some kid's getting the same I did?
I personally have seen body bags taken away
And it's not just someone died, it's more
Pretty England?

It scares the shit out of me!
Ungrateful?
I don't think I'll ever really know…
And that just knowing about myself
What have the drugs done to me?
Did I have the trip to do my book?
I don't know
Because I don't know any other state of mind
Is my mind just normal?

5 May 2006

Entertainment

You go to the cinema
You are looking to be entertained
Could you do the story?
How far are you willing to go?
Write a song?
Be a pop star?
I see so many ideas that have come from mental health
Ask yourself…
Mental hospitals
Is it just about making people well?

5 May 2006

III.iv

Put the Kettle On... 2006

Sunshine

A warm summer's day
Sunshine!
Changes your whole mood
Picks you up!
Winter, you expect it to be cold
Spring!
Flowers in your garden
Sunshine?
Give me the sun
Forever summer
Birds and bees
What more do you need?

6 May 2006

Forecast

National news
Local news
Followed by
National weather
Local weather
When do they get it right?
My forecast...
Open your curtains and have a look!

6 May 2006

Summer Cruising…

Summer cruising…
Windows down
It's the best!
Miles and miles
Which is a bit of a contradiction
Considering the pollution

6 May 2006

PC is a Killer!

Three, four, five years ago…
The Bungalow was a buzz!
Conversations?
You couldn't get a word in
PC – political correctness!
It's a killer…
A joke, a wrong word
And you may be asked to leave
The numbers have faded
But that could be anything?
PC?
It can't be good for people's well-doing
We dare not say a word
The Bungalow…
Surely is about letting your hair down
But!
No longer…

6 May 2006

This Is It, My All…

The image of Christ on the cross
To me, it's a man saying
'This is it, my all, what more do I have?'

It's any man, arms open wide
What more does he have?
We all have a cross
A burden!
A broken heart?
Loneliness?
Arms open wide…
This is it, a man, what more is there?

7 May 2006

When?

World on fire…
Why?
Motivation?
Yes, but where are we going?
Chillout…
Twentieth century technology
Do we need any more?
Twenty-first century
It's not just the money
Come on…
World peace?
Not just the oil
Step back, take a breath
The world?
How fantastic!
Enjoy it…
Not destroy it

7 May 2006

History?

Me, my poems…
My ideas, moods
History!
Just history
Me birthday this week

Will I still be writing in couple of years?
Very likely…
Each poem
I don't even read them
History?

7 May 2006

Tiger by the Tail

Dad was telling me about a recent dream
He had a tiger by the tail
And it turned and ripped him apart
It made me think about my poems
What if I do get the fame?
My kids think I'm a nobody
I know I'm not
Come on tiger…

7 May 2006

Attitude

If I am this Jesus guy?
Why ain't I everywhere saving people?
Jesus guy or not…
I'm only one person
I'm at the Bungalow trying to give people attitude
You need an attitude…
When you're on loads of meds and you've had knock after knock
You need something
Attitude?
It ain't in the social workers' book
It's all over!
My days are numbered
PC!

7 May 2006

Defrosting?

My guinea pigs…
One by one, a frozen block
The 1970s were cold
Also my pet dog taking them
He didn't always get fed
A young boy!
You grow cold to death, the ones you love…
My grandad being the final straw
But now!
Defrosting…
I get a lump in the throat
Just thinking…

7 May 2006

No Feelings

Sorry to keep talking about the meds
But it's important to me!
Part of my motivation for writing
Medication can take away your emotions
And with it your life…
When I saw my grandad in his coffin
Yes! It was upsetting
But I was cold, it didn't matter…
I was more upset because of my Uncle Richard and his wife being there
They were comforting me
And with the meds I never did grieve

7 May 2006

Remembering…

When my nan and grandad were alive
They were my world!
They still are my world

I see them every day in my mind
But when my nan lay dead in my mum's house
I hardly took a look
Wendy, my wife, was so upset
She was looking for and afraid of my reaction
Death ain't a problem for me
Is it the meds, was it my pets?
OK! Pets are not human
But I was a young boy and death is death
My nan and grandad are still with me
And always will be…

7 May 2006

Faith?

Those Bible stories?
The bread and the fish…
It's not about if it's true or not
It's about crossing the line of faith
And not always 'Jesus'
The faith within yourself
Some, most hear the stories
And just walk away
We all have the faith
We all know we have the faith
It's taking the time
But how many of us have the time?
I believe…
I believe in the magic!
Come on…
It's not about the truth
Faith?

8 May 2006

The Theme Tune to My Life

When I write a poem…
There is no point writing something that's already in my music collection

My illness or the medication
Gave me the paranoia to believe…
My music collection is all about me
Did I find the music or did my music find me?
The theme tune to my life
Is heaven-sent, really!
There is loads of evil
Even if it's just Hollywood, a story
Millions of different people
Different paranoias
If mine is heaven-sent?
What do others have?
The theme tune to my life…
It's no accident!

8 May 2006

Feeding…

When a singer writes a song
It's usually about themselves
And their paranoia, good or bad
The paranoia being their influences
And where they think it's going.
We're all feeding off one another's ideas
I believe some of the pop stars that are on drugs
Are actively looking for ideas in the paranoia.
I myself am in this paranoia game
But I was given the drugs without my consent
You know the rest…
I do have much more freedom
Because I ain't published
Yet?
Watch out!!!!!!!!!!!!

8 May 2006

What Do I know?

That last poem…
Drugs and paranoia?

It's not just about drugs!
I believe…
The biggest high is no drugs!
But hey!
What do I know?

9 May 2006

Journey's End!

Remember the ending?
The Wizard of Oz
Alice in Wonderland
Judy Garland could have gone home any time
And Alice was outside all the time
But for it to be over
You have to have got what you went there for
i.e. you have to believe…
Well? I can see the door
It's not so important any more
This 'Jesus' guy…
No more drugs!
And because I'm no longer suppressed
The need has gone
Journey's end?
I'm free!
And always was…

11 May 2006

Labyrinth

One of the all-time greats!
Labyrinth
With David Bowie and Jennifer Connelly
Believe me…
To be on a journey
Is so much better than no journey!
It's not just the knowledge
It's the magic!

Believing…
If you yourself are on such a journey
Always remember
'You have no power over me!'
The words near the end of the movie
Hell and back?
It's your life…

11 May 2006

Over to You!

You may have seen the movies
Understand every word!
You may read my poems
And again understand…
But if you don't get it?
Get it inside, life, life its very self

11 May 2006

A Glass of Water…

A glass of water…
A simple glass of water?
How fantastic!
I'm not talking about science
Just for an example
What might have scrambled your mind once
Is now your answer…
Without it ever changing even in your mind
Cheers!!!!!!!!!

11 May 2006

What's in a Name?

What is it?
Anything…

Because it's got a name
What's in a name?
i.e. 'chocolate', yes, we all know chocolate
But what is it?
Yes, they can break it down
But with more names...
Even nothing has a name...
'Nothing'

11 May 2006

Down the Line?

Disabled people
Twisted in wheelchairs
Drugs!
Somewhere down the line
Drugs...
One day...
Mental health and the physically handicapped
Will be a thing of the past
Not because they have found the answers, but
Because they have stopped looking

11 May 2006

Same Goal?

Watching the movie *Labyrinth*
With my girl, Karen,
Both in the mental health system
Tripping like crazy!
At times she would get quite frustrated with me;
I was on this journey
She wasn't, she already knew
So, watching the movie
We both saw and understood exactly the same concept
But had a difference in communication
And with it so many things in our lives
I remember, she thought I was a 'big kid'

So many husbands and wives fight over the same goal
Anyhow I would rather be in the movie
Than watching the movie…
Any time!

12 May 2006

Same Goal #2

My daughter and I
Have a similar problem with the movie *Labyrinth*
Sometimes the best communication
Is no communication…
At the end of the day!
The whole world has the same goal
Governments, pop stars, poets, soldiers and generals
When are we going to get it together?
Bin Laden, Bush standing next to each other?
Anyone standing next to each other?
Human's just standing there…
What's the problem?
Come on!

12 May 2006

Same Goal #3

It's only a problem
Because everybody makes it a problem

12 May 2006

Who's On Fire?

Take a man, trying to live his life, good or bad
Take a man trying to tell people how to live their lives
Who's on fire?
When you look around…
What do you see?

What you see is a reflection of yourself…
I see people having a laugh and trying to get on with their lives
Christians knocking your door
Who's on fire?

12 May 2006

Turn It Around…

Sex and violence
Where is it all going?
Ten years behind the USA…
Turn it around!
The media, TV
Make the US ten years behind us

12 May 2006

One Thousand Poems…

Why am I still writing?
I'm not saying anything new!
I'm bored
Bored with the way my mind works
Is this my last set of poems?
No more drugs
Time to get a life
If only it were that easy
I'm not bored with life
It's the poems!
I've no more to say
One-thousand poems…

12 May 2006

No Escape

I have a friend
He does not believe in Jesus Christ
And has never looked at a Bible
But with what need?
He has the enlightenment
From his own life, good or bad
Jesus may have been one of the first
But who has the copyright on enlightenment?
We all get it…
It's part of life
Good or bad?
No escape!

13 May 2006

Salvation

What is it to be saved?
Some would say 'The promise of eternity in heaven'
I believe it's closer to home…
To be saved is to be at peace with yourself
And the world you live in

14 May 2006

This Jesus Guy?

This Jesus guy…
Important?
Not important?
You tell me…

14 May 2006

The Best Poem in the World Ever!

Taking a break…
Get my life together without meds
Even if I get
The best poem in the world ever!
I ain't writing it
Not yet…

14 May 2006

Doors

Forty-six
One door closes
Another opens

14 May 2006

That Extra Mile

Extra mile?
I'm all out of extra miles
I'm not giving up!
I'm just beginning…
Now leave me alone?

15 May 2006

Spilling the Beans

Spilling the beans
Isn't everybody spilling the beans?
Some
Don't want you to have the beans
25p a tin
Down the local…

15 May 2006

Nothing…

Evolution?
God?
Adam and Eve?
Nothing…
Just think of nothing
This is not a cop-out
Because nothing is everything

15 May 2006

Stardust

The Big Bang?
So OK we're all stardust
But what is stardust?
You see?
Nothing…
But what is nothing?
Who's idea was this all?
Nobody's?
Just an idea…
Why?
And on and on and on…
Stop!
But I never started
Dot?
Dot ain't an answer

15 May 2006

Just Another Druggie

Fuck?
Just another druggie

15 May 2006

Cup of Tea

Answers?
We're all looking for answers
I've done my bit
But no more than anybody already knew
Put the kettle on…

15 May 2006

III.v

Back on the Chain Gang, 2006

Tug of War

One side…
The mental health system
The other side…
Life, including my music
One telling me it's an illness
The other telling me
I'm the Man!

21 May 2006

Youth Pill

Testing the pill
The pill to live for ever
But it is going to take for ever
To find out if it works

21 May 2006

For Ever?

Live for ever?
The magic pill
Live for ever?
Eternity in heaven
Live for ever?
I'm bored now…

21 May 2006

Back on the Chain Gang

Back on the meds…
Olanzapine 5mg
My mind was OK!
Oral facial tardive dyskinesia
The tongue
Just spins and spins

21 May 2006

Stop Writing?

Writing again?
I know, I know
I can't help myself
Stop writing
If only?
I'm addicted
If only I had something to write about

21 May 2006

Return to Oz

Twenty-odd years later
I took a trip back to Oz
My Oz being…
Letchworth and Stevenage
Rockabilly 1981
Where are you?
You broke my heart then…
You never learn!
Those girls
Return to Oz
There is no return to Oz…

25 May 2006

When Did It Start?

The Chosen One...
All this stuff in my head
When did it all begin?
Looking back
It was always there
These People, real people
Guiding me
Losing my Twin...
The Big Picture?
Where is it going?
And how does it end...?

25 May 2006

Arrogant

The Chosen One...
Does that make me arrogant?
If I am the chosen one?
It's you that have made me the chosen one
I write what I see
So if I am...
It's yours...

25 May 2006

Arrogant #2

Was, is Jesus Christ arrogant?
It's about looking beyond the words
When He said about the wine being his blood
What He was trying to say is...
Everything is made up of dust'
What He should have said is
The wine is everybody's blood

But still; does that make him arrogant?
He may have been leaving that for the future…

25 May 2006

Time Bomb?

All my life…
I've never been a drinker
Until now!
OK it's not a problem
2003, stopped the needle
Before I didn't need a drink
In my car
Yes! I'm in control
Time bomb…

25 May 2006

What Can You Do About It?

The end of the world…
Nuclear bombs
Walking through town
All eyes on you…
What can you do about it?
You can't control the action of others
Be happy
Get on…

25 May 2006

Time Bomb

The Cat Crept In

Cut Across Shorty…
Eddie Cochran
All these pop stars
Looking for their crown
The cat crept in
The last moment…
King of Kings
Last moment?
It was him all the time
The cat crept in…

25 May 2006

Make Your Mark

Make your mark
Live for ever
Make your mark
Dream that dream…
The King is dead!
Long live the King…
Make your mark
Live forever

25 May 2006

…In the Bank

King of Kings
Or not King of Kings?
Doesn't put the money
…in the bank
Being famous itself
Doesn't put the money in the bank
So when Jesus steps from the clouds
King of Kings or not?

Where's his money?
...in the bank
It ain't

25 May 2006

Anybody?

Sitting on the bus
Standing in a queue
Who is that next to you?
It could be anybody
Think about it, anybody...

25 May 2006

Polite Conversation

Polite conversation...
'What have you been up to?'
Reality, not a lot
In my mind, well...
Saved the planet time and time again
With my silly poems
Polite conversation
Sorry I asked

25 May 2006

Reflection

If you believe the world is bad
You will see the bad
If you believe the world is good
You will see the good
Also funny...
Happy, sad, a million things
Life can be a reflection
Think positive...

26 May 2006

The Hippy Dream

The late 1960s…
The hippy dream
LSD, peace, love
The Vision…
1960s just a boy…
Twenty-first century
Carrying the flag
Half the hippies run the country
The other half…
In…
The mental health system
The hippy dream?
It's to do with timing…

26 May 2006

Mobile Phones

Mobile phones
Who's listening?
In with the shrink
Social workers…
It's deliberate!
Paranoia…
Mobile phones
Anywhere?
Taking your photo
Video?
I don't know anyone without
A mobile
Apart from
Myself…

26 May 2006

Rush

My illness
Is my desire
Desire for life
Hey!
Why the rush?
I'm alive…

27 May 2006

What's It All About?

You spend all your life trying to work it out
One day it all falls into place
And you say to yourself
Why did I bother?
Some work it out young
Some never work it out
When you have your answers
You're no better off
Are you?

27 May 2006

One Million Dollars $$$

Foxton locks having a pint
Walking down the canal
A horse in a field
A sheep…
The sun is shining
The breeze is blowing
Put a million dollars next to the horse
What does he want with that?
He has everything he needs
The shepherd and the sheep?
The sheep only needs moving to another field

Because he's in a field to start with
Man may be intelligent
But we are all living creatures
OK, I don't want to live in a field
But man does make his own problems
When did you last see horses or sheep trying to kill one another?
One million dollars?
The horse would crap on it
One million dollars…
Give it to me!

27 May 2006

What Have We?

An old man
Sitting in front of the TV
It makes me sad
He's worked all his life
But ask yourself
What has any of us got?
Memories!
We've all got our memories
What have we?
Our life…
You don't know the man in front of the TV

27 May 2006

Big Wheel, Little Wheel

A king is nobody
Without his people
Big wheel, little wheel
Look inside a clock
It takes lots of little wheels
Take away even the smallest wheel
And Big Ben doesn't say ten!

27 May 2006

Access?

When I look at people
It's as if they know about me and my poetry
Sometimes my very latest ones…
Access?
Do they have access to my PC?
Or am I seeing that reflection?
My life…
Looking back at me

27 May 2006

How Many Frogs?

Looking for love…
Where's my prince?
Even a good-time girl
Where is he?

28 May 2006

Be Careful What You Wish For

Wishes do come true!
Be careful what you wish for
All those years ago…
I said about a new Bible
A lifetime of drugs and tripping
Even if they don't want my poems
I got my wish!
Be careful…

28 May 2006

Alpha Omega

Back in '99 I wrote
'Deep within there is nothing'
Alpha Omega
Millions of years back there was nothing
Millions of years to come…
There will be nothing again
But in that…
The nothing being everything
Just as it is
Deep within
Alpha Omega
Nothing…

28 May 2006

Alpha Omega #2

When you look within
What do you see?
Try to imagine the space that is the mind
Again it's nothing…
But that nothing being everything
My mind is my world
Inside out…
When I sleep
The darkness is blinding
Alpha Omega
There is nothing to understand
When you understand

28 May 2006

Fire?

Back in '84
Grafton Lodge, St Crispin's

After a nap
Forty winks…
I would jump up
Tear a page from a magazine
And set it alight
Why?
Still to this day I don't know
But…
I was never told off
Or asked about it
Imagine doing that these days…

28 May 2006

Getting Away With It

When you're crazy (ill)
You can and do
Get up to all sorts
Nobody seems to say much
But when you're well
The magic disappears
You know!
And so does everyone else

28 May 2006

My Love?

My love?
Is this it
On my own…?
Now I know!
Truly know
Is it too late?
You spend all your life
Learning the game
But you need another life
Knowing what you know
Fuck?

My love…
Is this it?

28 May 2006

Forward…

Rebels…
I'll tell you about the rebels!
It's the rebels
Who take it forward
I could have taken the drugs
And said thanks
Status quo
Fuck!
Where would you be?
Without
The rebels…

28 May 2006

Enjoy the Journey…

Out with friends
In my motor
Driving through the countryside
What we doing?
Where're we going?
Was all she said!
When we got back
She said how she enjoyed it
So?
Enjoy the journey…
Whatever you are doing
Don't wish your life away
Enjoy it…

29 May 2006

Open Your Eyes!

The air you breathe
The water you drink
Planet earth…
How fantastic!
Open your eyes
The wind and the rain
Sunshine…

29 May 2006

Suicide Bombers

Suicide bombers
All those virgins in heaven
I don't care how great heaven is
Give me planet earth!
For as long as possible
Always!

29 May 2006

Judgement Day?

What if we have already had our lives?
And what you are experiencing now is
Judgement Day!!!!!!!!!!?
I mentioned this to my daughter
And she said
'Where's the throne?'
My reply
Life, life itself
Is the throne!

29 May 2006

Chain Gang

Doing my time…
Writing these poems
Am I cursed?
Am I blessed?
All my life?
I don't know anything else

29 May 2006

Simple

My poems…
My poems are so simple
We all know the answers
It just needs someone to stand up and say

29 May 2006

III.vi

Size of a Cow, 2006

Special Effects?

Entertainment…
News at Ten
Special effects?
Real!!!!!!
Dead people

29 May 2006

Real World!

I could make a website
And give the world my poems
Unfortunately this is the real world
And I want the money

29 May 2006

Get Me Home…

News at Ten, tonight
US soldiers
Last November
Killing the innocent
It crossed my mind
Is this trying to get themselves home?
OK! they will be court-martialled
But
Does it get their mates home
Sooner…?

I don't presume to know
It just crossed my mind
Sorry!

30 May 2006

Fit?

Sitting here today…
I cannot foresee myself ever being in hospital again
But!
I can honestly say…
I am not physically able to do a week's work
Or mentally able
Fit?
If I went to work
I would end up setting myself alight
With…
What I think is
Stress!!?

30 May 2006

Fit? #2

What is the point?
Of being in bed with a really fit girl
If you are rubbish?

30 May 2006

Geldof

Tell me why
I don't like Geldof
I don't know the man
But…

Tell me why
Joke!

31 May 2006

Plant

I believe
Some of my ideas and poems
Have been deliberately planted in me
Sometimes by saying the opposite
Or is it just me?
Life…

31 May 2006

The Size of a Cow

How do you eat a whole cow?
How do you understand Colin?
A burger at a time
A poem at a time

31 May 2006

The Holy Grail

Drinking from the cup
The Holy Grail…
The giver of life!
A woman's womb
The virgin's pussy

31 May 2006

Dark Side of Rock 'n' Roll?

Did Buddy Holly sign his own death certificate?
The small print…

So he had to get it all in, in three years!
Jerry Lee Lewis marrying his cousin
The small print?
Testing the boundaries

1 June 2006

Words…

I once heard it said on the TV that
The Bible is just the propaganda of its day
Well…
If my book ever becomes anything
I just wish to set people free!
Those who are looking to be set free?
Also confirming
What most already know…
If you have a shitty job?
You will likely still have that job
I only have some words
You know the rest…

1 June 2006

Lemmings

Lemmings running over the cliff
In theory…
It just takes one to say stop
In theory?

1 June 2006

How Simple Do You Want It?

Meriel, my social worker
Once said to me
'It's not that simple, is it!'
My reply was

'How simple do you want it?'
We were talking about my poems…

1 June 2006

Lyrics

Lyrics?
It doesn't matter how good your lyrics are
If nobody's listening

3 June 2006

Really Don't Get It!

Amanda and Jez's wedding today!
Church of Christ the King, Kettering
Listening to members of my family
Some really don't get it!
It was said about 'Love'
These members of my family are supposed to be in love
With their partners?
Love is life itself
Bring God into the equation
And it's a joke!
God is Love is Life…
It's in all of us
Some
Really don't get it!

3 June 2006

She Really Don't Get It!

My daughter!
She really don't get it…
God!
Or
The idea of God

Is the same!
Maybe I'm closer?
Because I'm not reading from an old book
I'm in touch today
My daughter and I
Are batting for the same team
She cannot see it
If my daughter and I can't get it together
What hope is there for the world?
Maybe we're too close?
The wood for the trees...

3 June 2006

On My Own?

I believe many have this feeling
Love, life, the universe
Which I choose to call 'God'
Am I on my own?
Many don't seem to recognise
The 'God' bit...
On my own?
Too many drugs?
Whatever...

4 June 2006

The Little Guy?

Democracy?
Looking after the little guy
Millions are spent on the emergency services
Sometimes for one person!
Contradiction isn't it?
The thousands sent off to war...

4 June 2006

Waiting for My Man

Couple of nights ago
I gave Mac and Will a copy of my poems
I hope they got the discs
The packet was taken from the stage
Waiting for my man
'Mac'
Realistically I don't expect anything
But?

4 June 2006

When?

When?
In your own time?
When you're young?
When?
Knowledge?
It's not just knowledge
Feelings
Believing…
To truly understand?
Like anything
You have to find it yourself
When?

5 June 2006

Temptation

That little devil…
Temptation!
Credit cards?
The shops full of goodies
It's not just about evil!
God, Jesus…

Is also full of it!
Temptation?
How far are you willing to go?
A lifetime of poems
How far…

5 June 2006

The Wall

The Wall…
Do I have the final brick?
Is there a final brick?
I believe
Writing these poems
Is that brick!
But!
To be published
Is to knock it all down
And…
About time!

5 June 2006

Terms

Natalie said to me that
I want God, but on my terms
Well sorry Natalie
But you are no different
If God were God
We wouldn't have all these different faiths
At least my idea
Tries to bring everybody together
We will see…
I don't see your faith bringing anybody together
Unless?
It's your terms…

5 June 2006

Harsh Words

Harsh words!
I hear you say
Well?
Imagine if or when my book takes off
I have a vision
The stakes are high
Daughter or not
I can't back down now!
If she truly cannot see what's in front of her
Well?
I have no more words
There aren't the words…

5 June 2006

Two Things!

Saturday the wedding…
I noticed two things
How to be humble
Dad backing down from Jez
But!
The other…
No fucker
Backed down at my wedding!
I'll tell
When I can be bothered

5 June 2006

If?

If you believe
Someone is watching you
That's paranoia
Right!

But if they really are watching
Then it's not paranoia
Because it's real
Right!
My illness
My vision
Is my paranoia
But if it is real?
I'm not ill
And never was
Right!

5 June 2006

Six Six Six

Today!
Sixth June '06
666
Demon's day
The Omen
Released at the cinema
It's all rubbish
Just numbers
Some have nothing better to do
The Devil?
Come on I say
It will be a laugh
666
Seven the number for God
Just numbers…

6 June 2006

If? #2

Next time you're dishing out the pills
Shoving the needle in
Find out if what they are saying is true

6 June 2006

Gambling?

Pastor Pavitt and his Church
Look down on gambling
What if God wanted to reward me?
A million pounds isn't going to fall from the sky
A pound on the Lotto?
Doesn't Pavitt deserve a wad?

7 June 2006

Disagree

It is human nature to disagree
Even if I find all the right words
Some will still disagree
Take Elvis
For every one fan
He had two that disliked him
Disagree?
Hey!
I'm happy…

8 June 2006

Iran?

Iran…
Do we need any more trouble?
Haven't we got enough to sort out?
The second coming…
Man will still argue!
Disagree…
Iran?
Come on boys
Get it together…

9 June 2006

Boys Will Be Boys

JCB
Digging up the road
A nice motor car
Intercity 125
Guns and killing
Bombs
Nuke the world?
Boys will be boys…

9 June 2006

Want It!

Wanting it isn't enough
You could write a million poems
You have to go and get it!
How?
Where?
My illness tells me
Everybody already knows…
So?
Just…
So!

10 June 2006

Pat on the Back, Not

Saving the planet
Poem after poem…
Not a thank you!
No pat on the back!
Money?
I've got me social…
'Saving the planet'

What actually does that mean?
I don't know?
Pat on the back, not

10 June 2006

Believing

Believing
Just believing
Is better than
Not believing
What have you
Without belief?

10 June 2006

One Day?

One day?
One day soon
I would like to be somebody
With my poems!
I am already that person
The poems are written
One day!
Soon…

10 June 2006

Five Years?

Some do say…
If you set out to get somewhere
You will probably never get there
Well?
Five years' time
I wish to be off my sofa
Living the dream!

Instead of
Dreaming it…

10 June 2006

The Girl Thing?

I need to get it together!
This girl thing?
If I don't sort myself out
I'm always going to be on my own
I'm not ugly
A bit fat
I need some words…
Hey!
Aren't you the poet?
The girl thing?
You know!

10 June 2006

My Favourite Subject

I've been a reading my poems
My favourite subject
Seems to be…
'The End' of my poems
No more ideas!
Well?
It's not the end of my poetry
But like before
It feels like it…

10 June 2006

III.vii

My Way… 2006

Wall of Vision?

Wall of vision?
Yes, we all know about the eyeballs
Yes, we all know there's a brain…
Wall of vision…
Five-foot six-inches from the ground
Where does it start?
What's behind
Wall of vision?
Walking around…

11 June 2006

Dynamo

The human body…
Electricity?
Where is the dynamo?
If you are a doctor…
A medical student?
You likely know the answer
But for a poet?
Electricity?
Love…
The earth!
One big dynamo…

11 June 2006

Wall of Vision? #2

Close your eyes…
And you see darkness
But you have the vision to see the darkness!
I have never spoken with a blind person
But without vision
Do you see nothing?
What does nothing look like?

11 June 2006

Vision of Nothing

I have a vision of nothing
Alpha Omega
It's a vision of an empty void
Darkness but not!
You and I
Should
Count our blessings…

11 June 2006

Mother

My mother
All this time
The crazy one!
Years of drugs and shit
There it was
Mother!
Recently many have told me
It was she
But like anything
You have to find it yourself
To believe…
I don't have the words

She must know
The umbilical cord has been cut
My mother
The woman who gave me life
So many memories
Mum
I love you
xxx

12 June 2006

Untitled #2

My mother…
Knows one thing
I may never know…
Dad?
What my dad looks like…
Those eyes?
My father…

12 June 2006

Some Answers?

My boy!
Has some of the answers
The way he holds himself
Etc.
I try to imagine…
A seventy-year-old man
Not unlike me and my boy
Why?
When?
If ever…

12 June 2006

Together…

If you read a poem
And it makes no sense at all
Read on…
The next few may enlighten you
If I don't feel I have explained myself
I have a few stabs
Several poems
Together…

12 June 2006

Armageddon…

Armageddon…
The end of the world?
Sorry!
Cancelled
Man isn't that stupid
And the sun?
A few million years yet

13 June 2006

Brainwashed?

All you idiots
Blowing yourselves up
And I think I'm brainwashed?
Hey!
Give it to me!

13 June 2006

No More Tears!

No more looking for answers
No more tears…
Turning yourself inside out
OK?
The dream is not yet fulfilled, but
No more tears…
Maybe
Tears of joy?

15 June 2006

Why Wait?

It's common sense
The oil is going to dry up.
Forget the politics.
Who gets the money!
We have the technology –
Make a new method of transport
Today!
Why wait?

15 June 2006

Necessity…

Necessity…
The mother of invention!
When the oil has gone
You know…
Again!
Why wait?

15 June 2006

Nobody?

I feel that my time is close
Destiny is a calling…
But…
If I am to be a nobody
I need to know
So I can settle down
And be just that

16 June 2006

Fantasy?

Living day-to-day
With meds!
I dream…
I trip…
Life is a fantasy…
If my dreams did come true
It would just be more of the same
I'm already in that dream
But
If they don't
I will always have this longing
Fantasy?

16 June 2006

Uncool is Cool!

In your teens and twenties
It's important to be cool
There comes a point you discover
It's all bullshite

Cool is uncool
And vice versa…

18 June 2006

Not for Sale!

Luke, my dear boy
One day…
You will realise
Blood is thicker than water.
My boy
Not for sale!
And I'm not buying him…

19 June 2006

Local Rock 'n' Roll

The local rock and roll scene
Same people
Same music
All the time!
The bands
Same songs
Different people.
OK, rock 'n' roll is fifty years old
But they're not even trying.
If it were original
The locals would walk out.
I took a couple of weeks out
Went back
No different!
Local rock and roll…
It ain't worth the bother.
Bollocks?

19 June 2006

Memories…

The good ol' days…
Memories are made of this
Nick Willett
Northampton January '06
Happy days
Never ending
Tenth Rockabilly Rave
Caister '79
Memories…

19 June 2006

Folsom Prison Blues

Yes! We need law and order
Yes! We need prisons
But
What gives one man
The right to tell another…?

20 June 2006

No Angel For Me?

I've done me poems!
I'm all out of poems…
The girl…
No angel for me?
I've asked!
What more?
There is no more!!!!!!!!!

21 June 2006

Not Just Two Sides…

Is it an illness and not real?
Is it real?
The Chosen One!
Not just a two-sided battle.
Just as I feel my daughter understands
She doesn't!
My music collection…
I've explained many times!
But still
No one has said 'Yes!' in my face
But if they did
I would still have the battle.
In the film
Walk the Line
His dad grabs the radio and says
'This is nothing!!!!!!!'
Over one-thousand poems!
And I agree
It's nothing!
My mind is a battlefield
Not just two sides…
Many!

21 June 2006

Come the Day!

Come the day!
The world gets my poems
Famous!
Sitting in my farmhouse
Yes! Yes!
I do hope so
It isn't nothing!
But ask Bono about his millions…

You see?
It is nothing

21 June 2006

My Way…

Hell and back!
Ripped my insides apart
Flew with the angles…
Drank from the cup
Crucified!
A million needles
What do we have?
Any of us…
The moment!
We have the moment
The past has gone!
The future yet to come
Hell and back?
The Holy Grail…
My way…

21 June 2006

Big Apple!

Life?
Life is one big apple!
Have you had your bite?
God may have said
Leave my tree alone
But we are no longer in the garden
And life is for living…

21 June 2006

Reborn…

My time is close
So many waiting
Reborn?
To be reborn
Is to be understood
Accepted…
But also
To accept yourself
Fulfil the dream?
Then
And only then
Reborn…

23 June 2006

I Want It Back!

Time to face the world…
I always knew what I was writing
But I was writing in innocence
I want it back!
Time to face the world!

26 June 2006

Fed Up

Fed up…
My music?
My music isn't doing it
TV?
The TV is always rubbish
My PC
Takes forever
Me poems
Is it next year…?

Fed up
Fed up
Fed up

26 June 2006

The Monster?

The monster?
He's very quiet these days
The low before the storm…
The meds?
Maybe the meds are working
If I am to face the world
I will need him…
I think?
Shhhhhhhh
Maybe he's asleep
The monster…
Within

26 June 2006

Me Millions £££

The last year or so
I've asked a couple of girls out
Nothing!
Negative…
When, if
I get me millions £££
What then?
I've already asked!
If I wasn't good enough then…

26 June 2006

True

Back in '84
With a pill on my tongue
Listening to
Morrissey, McCulloch
All night long
I know this much is
True!

27 June 2006

Care in the Community

Back in the eighties
Being in hospital...
Mental hospital
You not only had your problems
You had everybody's.
Of course you talked with each other
Loads of vibes
Sensitive and fragile
It was a melting pot!!!!!!!
The meds kicking in.
Once I had this girl inside me, spiritually
Crazy shit!
Crazy times!
Today?
Care in the community.
I'm all for
Care in the community
Until some idiot
Blows it!

27 June 2006

Rolling

I can write the poem
No problem!
The business side
Help!
Pastor Pavitt
Is looking into that at the moment
Realistically
He is my only hope
Rolling?
If the ball isn't rolling in 2007
Cobwebs!
The spiders will get the lot
It's not about giving up
It's about being realistic

27 June 2006

Laughing at You

Some who don't believe
Never looked at a Bible
Laugh at Jesus
But yet
Have the enlightenment, life!
Well, Jesus
Is laughing at you!
You fool!
God is life
The joke is you!

28 June 2006

Fat Git

Considering…
I'm on Olanzapine

Gave up smoking
Me age!
I ain't doing too bad
In the fat git department
Look at…
Elvis
Jim Morrison
Two of the biggest sex symbols
In the world…
It gets us all, usually
Don, my dad
It missed him…

28 June 2006

Nigel Lewis

Nigel Lewis!
One of the founders of psychobilly
Song after song
Showing me the way
Getting me started!
The Tall Boys!
'Moving Staircases'
It's not always about being famous
Sometimes it's…
Who you influence…
But if I were to list all my influences
Well?
Anyway!
Nigel Lewis…
This Saturday 1st of July
Yesssssss!!!!!!!!

28 June 2006

Influences?

OK, influences?
Everybody influences everybody!

Someone you've never met
The knock-on effect!
Someone you don't like!
Someone you like?
Music…
Not just the lyrics, the trip
At school
When you're young
Everything…
It is impossible not to be influenced
Good or bad?

28 June 2006

Heights

I am not afraid of heights
When I am actually there
I can stand at the top of the car park
No problem!
It's when I'm in bed
Thinking about it
I put myself into situations
With heights
And get a shooting pain
In my shins
When it enters my head
It's hard to think of something else
Goodnight!
There it is again…

28 June 2006

Liar?

I'm not one for counting sins
But
To be a liar
Has to be near the top!
When you do tell the truth

No one will believe you
And if you are a liar
You won't believe anybody else
You may as well give up talking
Liar! Liar!
Pants on fire…

28 June 2006

III.viii

Kingdom Come, 2006

Fame Game?

When, if, I hit the big time
What I will be famous for will be history
In the past!
My book
My poems
May make me famous
But what I'm writing about
Is in the past…
But I wasn't famous then
When I should have been
I hadn't written it then
But that is when I was truly famous
Understand?
Fame game?

29 June 2006

Fame Game #2

Years ago…
When I was banged up in hospital
All the feelings
The trip!
The TV
The radio
I just wanted out!
So I could be this famous guy.
In hindsight

What would I have been famous for?
I hadn't written my book

29 June 2006

Actually

The Church of 'Jesus Christ'
Isn't actually
The Church of Jesus Christ!
It's the Church of
The people who put the Bible together.
How many different versions do we have?
Even the original
King James Version
Has to be about those who put it together.
You all know my story
I looked for the Jesus within
Am I adding to the confusion?
Or helping to sort it out…
Time will tell?

30 June 2006

Stop the Killing!

Gaza
Palestinian
Bush, Blair
Whoever is in office
Bin Laden…
If you are reading this
STOP THE KILLING!!!!!!!!!!!
Lay down your guns!
Any fucker
Lay 'em down
Are you stupid?
Are your lives that boring?

Take a deep breath
Stop the killing!

30 June 2006

Fame Game #3

Of course
What I may be famous for
Today and in the future…
Is passing it on

2 July 2006

When?

Every three seconds
A child dies in Africa from poverty
It's not the money
It's the politics
Politics?
I don't know
I don't want to know
I don't need to know
When?
When is the world going to wake up
We could send all our money
The lot!
A child would still die
Every three seconds
Politics
When?

2 July 2006

Band Aid

Music is my life
Listening to music

Band Aid?
I have never directly given them money
Why?
I'm not bothered about the politics
Why?
It doesn't add up!
Guilty?
No I don't feel guilty

2 July 2006

Bono

All those years ago when Bob was swearing
And telling you to give the shirt off your back
Did Bono empty his bank account?
The paradox!
Bono and his like
Made millions indirectly because of Band Aid
Also, no matter how many people know about Bono
and his AIDS/HIV campaign
Yes! People need to know
But again!
It's the politics…
We all know this don't we?
I love Bono
Take a look at my U2 collection
Sort the politics out…
PS I'm not telling Bono to stop!

2 July 2006

Christmas?

Band Aid?
Bob, Bono
The little guy with his £10
Bush, Blair etc.
Dealing in their zillions
What's going on?

What are we waiting for
Christmas?
Even Jesus is just one guy…

2 July 2006

Why the Blast?

Why the blast of 'Band Aid' poem?
It was on the TV
I was changing a DVD and there it was!
Bob, Bono, Beckham
Clicking their fingers every three seconds
Picking on the little guy!!!!!!!!
Fuck off!

2 July 2006

My Voice!

Yes it wasn't about money
It was your voice
Well here is my voice
'Beckham and what he represents' clicking his fingers about a kid dying
Sucks!
Big time!
If you think I've got a problem?
Yes!
I very likely have…

2 July 2006

Next…

Next!
We will have Blair and Cameron
Clicking their fingers every three seconds
Revolution?
I'll give you a revolution!!!!!!!!!

The Joke?
I haven't said anything anybody don't already know!!!!!!!!!

3 July 2006

Sight Savers

I personally give a small amount
To Sight Savers
Monthly direct debit
I always tick the box 'no mail'
They probably spend more money
Than what I give
Asking me for more…!

3 July 2006

Kingdom Come!

The Kingdom of God
The Kingdom of heaven
Kingdom come!
Open your eyes and you are there…

3 July 2006

World on Fire?

The burning preacher
Who can't save himself.
The sinner
Who can't see his sins.
The prison guard
Locked in prison.
The sailor
Lost at sea.
World on fire?
Open your eyes
It's that simple…

And you are there!
Believe…

3 July 2006

My Boy!

My boy
Sixteen this year
A smoker!
Like anyone he has to find out himself
My boy
His whole life in front of him
Some things go unspoken…
Does he see what I see?
Like anything?
You have to find it yourself
My boy!

3 July 2006

King's Cross

'88 London
King's Cross fire
Several months later
Middle of a breakdown
Going down the escalators
Smoking me fags!
'Put that fag out!'
Many shouted
Sometimes you have to test the boundaries
Not sure how?
But still!
So much stuff on TV
You have to go exploring…
Giving up the fags
One of the best things I ever did!

3 July 2006

Forbidden Fruit?

For those with open eyes…
The forbidden fruit
May very well be the misuse of drugs
For the biggest high is being straight
Maybe?
Some have a long way to go

3 July 2006

Forbidden Fruit #2

Some say
That the forbidden fruit is
To be gay…
Well, Adam and Eve weren't gay.
Some say
It is to have another's love you shouldn't –
Where does that leave Adam and Eve?
There was nobody else
Forbidden fruit?
Is it just love
How I wish for some on my table…
Love?

3 July 2006

My Eyes #2

All those years ago
Twenty-two years!
I wrote the poem
'My Eyes'
I could see the kingdom
But I wasn't in
Money would be nice
But it's not just the money

It's about being,
Knowing who you are
You may be King of England
But if you don't know yourself and who you are?
Forget it!
The being
In human being
Your psyche
Soul, spirit, you!
There is no key
Open your eyes
And you're in…

3 July 2006

Your Voice!

I am not a pop star!
I'm not a singer
These poems
Are your poems
Read them in your head
Your voice!

3 July 2006

Psychobilly?

Psychobilly?
What is psychobilly…
Firstly it's music!
Music that in most sings about 'hell'
But being a reject of hell
In most…
Most just don't understand!
It's a dark way of saying you're good
'Psychobilly'
Covers many topics, no rules
What makes it powerful to me
Is its roots in the fifties

Many of the original rockabillies are dying off
And psychobilly
Is making them spin in their graves
Keeping the party going
Who's going to make the psychobillies spin?
In a few words
That's psychobilly!

3 July 2006

What's Going On?

Turn on your telly
It's not a perfect world
But would a perfect world work
Man needs a bit of blood
In this?
Is the West trying to sort it out
Or helping it along?

3 July 2006

The Side Room!

Locked up in hospital
The side room
Full of drugs
Hate drugs
I've been there
One of the good guys
What happened to those
Who didn't come up?
Paul Rogers one, 1988
'Love' I dared

3 July 2006

Save the Tiger!

If I am to save the planet
Whatever saving the planet is
Memories
So many people!
If I ain't doing it for myself
I can't let so many down
So many?
That's everybody!

3 July 2006

100%

My poems may not be
100% Christian
But I believe the message is

5 July 2006

No Promises?

The Ring?
Lord of the Rings...
If my words
Are the Ring
To destroy them
Is to give them back.
The world, you!
Gave me the poems.
It's a long journey
With little reward
Or at least...
Until the job is done.
But still
No promises?

6 July 2006

Listen Here!

Is it you?
Are you the one?
One-thousand years from now!
I have been driven by desire
You should not!
Listen here!
Remember…
All or nothing!

6 July 2006

My Star Wars!

We named my son Luke
Inspired by the movie
Star Wars
Well?
If Luke my son is Skywalker
That must make Natalie Princess Leia
But!
In my *Star Wars*
Darth Vader did save the universe

6 July 2006

Three Young Men

This week at
Pastor Pavitt's church
Three young men
From Crown College USA
So passionate about Christ
And the Bible
Now?
Are they passionate about the Word
Or about the concept?

I don't wish to knock any of it
But some of it is so not true!
But the concept yes!!!!!
The spirit is in us all…

6 July 2006

Human Spirit?

I have always said
The spirit of Jesus is in us all
What if it ain't Jesus?
Only the 'human spirit'
Some choose to describe it as Jesus
And some don't
But have the same feelings
When walking through town
I see the spirit
Before I see the person
Human spirit?

7 July 2006

Blind?

Most Christians would say
The unbeliever is blind
What if
It is the Christian that is blind?
Basically its comes down to words
We are all human!
With similar feelings…

7 July 2006

The Teacher

Good and bad?
Jesus and the Devil?
Basically it's a story
And how and where you learn it
Some feel the need
To pass it on…

7 July 2006

Judgement

If this is Judgement Day
Everybody is
Judging everybody…

7 July 2006

Same?

I have it on DVD
Ray Manzarek saying
'A Doors concert is like a religious experience'
Most people have never had a religious experience
Most people are not Christian!
So how can Ray make the comparison?
And the Christians
Believe that they have the copyright
On all that stuff…
At the end of the day
We are all human, and yes
With similar feelings
Once the world recognises this
We may start to get somewhere
That's everybody!

7 July 2006

Thinking?

Take one guy
Standing next to another guy
Both of them
Not thinking about much
The problem comes
When they try to imagine
What the other may be thinking
On the world stage
For example?

7 July 2006

Freedom/Mental Illness

Freedom can be
Staring at the wall in your home
If you haven't many friends
With similar interests;
But that's mental illness.
Looking at a brick wall?
Freedom?
What is freedom…?
I ain't free?
Freedom is about choice
Is it?

8 July 2006

What to Do?

What to do?
OK, I'm not educated
I've been there…
Alpha Omega
Heaven and hell
It's not about education!

The girl?
There is no girl
What to do?
This 'Jesus' stuff?
It's just a story...
If you want me to be Jesus
I'll be Jesus!
What to do?
Come on!

8 July 2006

Suicide?

When it's your time
It's your time!
Suicide?
I'm worth more than suicide!
Ninety miles per hour
Back from Leicester!
Not this time!
When?

8 July 2006

III.ix

Walking Forward... 2006

China

1988 she said
China in your hands
Don't push too hard!
1993 I'm pushing
Pushing my hardest
Packing crisps in '88
1993 open all doors!
She said
Don't push too hard
I'm pushing
Pushing my hardest!

14 May 1993

The Dead Stay Dead

The dead stay dead
Apart from those in your head
Cast those demons out
Set your angels free
The dead stay dead
Apart from those in your head

4 January 1998

Turkey

I feel like a turkey
Sitting here
Without a thought
Without inspiration
I feel like a turkey
A prize turkey

8 December 1999

Loner

A bit fed up…
A bit lonely
I'll give 'Mead-Hurst' a ring…
Before I've even picked the phone up…
I have my Answers?!!!
A bit fed up indeed…
The very fact I have my answers
Makes me fed up…
A bit fed up…
A bit lonely
…indeed

1 February 2004

Without Love

If I had someone to love
I'd likely forget all that Jesus crap…
(Sorry, the real Jesus)
I don't do anything!
I don't go down the local…
No girl is going to knock my door
I'm apathetic about the whole thing

Can't be bothered
The kiss I'd die for…
Without love…

2 February 2004

Magic?

The wind blowing through the trees
The stars that shine at night
Sunshine…
That's magic…
A rabbit from a hat!
No… not really
The sweet smell of your perfume
Your soft, gentle voice
Your hands down my back
Oh yes…
Magic!

17 February 2004

1974

Standing on the corner in my new blue jeans
Dreaming about the girl in my limousine
Showaddywaddy 1974
It hasn't stopped
Those thumping drums…
Twanging guitars
Forty-four this year!
And still dreaming…

24 February 2004

Wall of Silence

You empty your brains…
Give them the world!

You never learn
Years of seeing the shrink
All your life, just a boy…
You never learn
Next week another appointment
You can't help yourself
What do you get for your troubles?
The title of this poem.

4 March 2004

Love Is… #2

Love is…
Lying in bed, farting! And…
Pulling the covers over her head!
Love is…
Not saying anything
Sometimes it's not what you do
But what you don't do…
Heck!
What do I know?
I'm divorced…

5 April 2004

Fuck Off and Die!

Tell the lady
I said goodbye…
Tell the lady
Fuck off and die!
Tell the lady
I said goodbye…

20 April 2004

Alive

Alive?
I know that I'm alive
I can hear the birds a-singing
Singing for you and me

20 May 2004

The Remains of the Day

Freedom?
The butler
Was still a butler

13 October 2004

Judgement

We all have skeletons…
Who's keeping a record?
Come judgement…
It's all within

6 November 2004

Down the Road

Enlightenment
Spirituality
Equality
Knowing your neighbour
Knowing you share…
Enlightenment
Spirituality
That must be the road

The right road
Give it a go?

29 January 2005

On Your Toes

Sitting in the town
Having a cup of tea
Arthur says…
'Looks like rain'
But the sun comes out!
That's God for ya
Keeping ya
On your toes…

13 March 2005

Damaged Goods

Me, myself
Damaged
Damaged goods!
But I do believe
Because of that
I have much more to give

1 July 2005

Time for Bed

Who you are?
What you are?
'Time for bed'
Can mean many different things
Nightmares?
Fun?
Let's run…

25 July 2005

Alone?

Alone?
Maybe I'm meant to be alone
Sitting here bored
A friend visits me
I can't wait for them to leave
Just to be…
Alone?

14 August 2005

Poetry in Motion?

Poetry in motion?
Bollocks!
It's all crap…

1 September 2005

Who?

Who are they shouting at?
You?
Me?
Relax man…
No need to shout

10 October 2005

Arguing

A day spent arguing
Is a day wasted

14 October 2005

Time

They say…
Everything has its time and place!
My time?
Is now…
But my words
Will always have a time!

29 November 2005

Tears?

How many?
How many tears?
Turning yourself inside out

16 December 2005

What If…

What if…
It really is me
Inspired all these pop stars!
What if…
It really was me
They were talking about on the TV?
Does it
Automatically follow
I'm going to be loaded one day?

9 July 2006

Time Out

Did you notice the dates?
Time out

The last few poems
Back to today
Back to the future
Time out

9 July 2006

Education

My music!
My DVD collection
Is my education
So OK I'm educated!
What now?

9 July 2006

Ignorance is Bliss?

Once you know!
I mean really know…
Are you any better off?

10 July 2006

Boring Old Man?

Very recently an old friend said
You're still going?
(Me poems)
You've not became a boring old man…?
Well?
Next week in with the shrink
I wanna talk about coming off the meds
This Jesus guy?
Maybe I've already been this Jesus guy
We will see.
For the moment

I just wanna be this
Boring old man…

12 July 2006

Forgive

Before I can fall in love
Before I can let myself fall in love
I have to forgive all those who have broken my heart
But also!
I have to forgive myself
So many bitter people
We have to move on
I have to move on!
How?
This isn't just words
Forgive?

13 July 2006

The Power!

When I say
'God' is an idea in your head
I don't just mean
Think of the word 'God'
Think of the power of the idea
Then?
You (we) maybe getting somewhere?
The power!

14 July 2006

Crossroads/What If?

All those years ago!
That crossroads/what if?
1980 entering the mental health system

We all contain a fire!
No secret, some need pills
Would I have run myself into an early grave?
What if?
A different road…
We only get the one shot (life)
Have I blown it?
Was it meant to be?
We will see…

16 July 2006

Walking Forward…

Walking forward…
Forward with Christ!
We may not always agree
But we are together!
I haven't come all this way
To give up now!
Forward…
Forward with Christ!
Always…

16 July 2006

Goal?

Goal?
Have I done what I set out to do?
A new 'Bible'
Maybe?
But for the most…
I was just doing some poems
The Christians have their book
And the non-Christians don't want a book
My journey is nearing a close
Whatever the outcome

I did my best
Goal?
You tell me…

16 July 2006

Already Happened

All you non-believers
Waiting for the 'second coming'
Don't you get it?
It's here! It's now!
It's already happened
OK you are not all in church
Singing 'Onward Christian Soldiers'
It's the enlightenment!
Good or bad?
You've all got it
It's been in your TV for years!
Your music?
Open your eyes and take a listen…
You drunks
Why do you think you're drunk?
Enlightenment…
Turn the key!
And be free…

16 July 2006

The Blockbuster Dream

I have just awoken from a dream, a dream which I have had many times many different ways! To cut to the chase:

The world doesn't need saving and never did! The world, and the people in it, need to save those who find the need!

Elvis sang the song about the world being a stage… anyway, back to the dream.

I am in the Millennium Dome walking around my own film set. Bono and the boys (U2) are doing the music. I don't like water so the set is aboard ship. Basically I save the world and the world saves me!

Lots of action!

Dreaming the blockbuster dream! This time I'm making a note.

What I'm saying is, my life is one big film set for me to save the world because I find the need, which means the world is saving me!

Entertainment!

The world needs entertainment…

Last Action Hero, Schwarzenegger

The Truman Show, Jim Carrey

A million films! But this is my life and yes my dream…

Tell me, when Truman broke through, did they carry on filming him?

I have just had the dream, this is all so real to me at the moment, I didn't say much about the dream…

More the concept!

17 July 2006

Save?

Did Jesus Christ save us?
Or
Did we save Him?

17 July 2006

On Fire!

How do you set someone on fire?
Talk about them!
My ears are burning…

17 July 2006

Saved!

They say when you are saved
The spirit of Jesus enters into you
Well, I was saved back in '79–'80
But without the knowledge of the Bible
My knowledge?

Sex, drugs and rock 'n' roll!
But still
Jesus was with me…
Saved!!!!!!!!

17 July 2006

Choice!

When my daughter says
She believes every word in the Bible
But also that God gave us a mind of our own
i.e. 'choice'
To believe the Bible or not!
But then to make the choice black and white
Believe everything in it or not?
Is to take away that choice!
So many will never have a choice about the Bible
Because they believe
Their choice?
Is never to look at one

17 July 2006

III.x

Regardless, 2006

What Is It?

Mental illness
What is it?
I can only comment from my own experiences
Well?
It is in all of us
The fire!
A desire for life, the lust
What to do?
With this inferno
Slow down!
The fire
The fire burns…

18 July 2006

Control?

Mental illness
The illness is a trip
So you get the meds
And make a bigger trip
To override the illness
Then you are on a controlled trip
Until?
The trip that is the illness
Disappears…
That's
How I see it

18 July 2006

Unnecessary…

I believe
Millions of people
Are on unnecessary meds
Because they can't tell the difference between
The trip that is the illness and
The trip that is the meds!

18 July 2006

Adam and Eve?

Do I believe in Genesis,
Adam and Eve…?
I believe in the idea
The story
The concept!
The reality?
Well, not really…
If you believe in evolution
Well?
Where did evolution start, with
Adam and Eve?
So many different races
I don't believe we all came from the same seed!
Many, Adam's and Eve's
Maybe?

18 July 2006

Evolution?

Evolution?
I don't believe the earth is old enough
For life to have come from
A 'cell' in the water.
Adam and Eve,

God
Seems far more logical

18 July 2006

Wise?

Wise?
Don't be in a rush
It's not all it's cracked up to be

20 July 2006

Too Late?

Hot summer's day!
Glorious sunshine…
Turns cold
Too late?
Thinking…
Why didn't I make the most of it?

21 July 2006

Boy Racer!

All those years!
Putting my foot down
All those years!
Boy racer…
Where did I think I was going?

23 July 2006

Four Types of Music

Good music
Bad music

Music I like
Music I don't

25 July 2006

Hungry?

I heard on the radio
Some years back
It is more natural to feel a bit hungry
Than full all the time. So
Next time you're running to the fridge
Slow down man…

25 July 2006

Stick To Your Guns…

It's not all about straight As
Top of the class!
A kind heart…
Goes a long way
If you know what I'm saying?
Stick to your guns…

25 July 2006

Troubled Times…

Kicking the habit!
Friends giving you a hard time?
Focus!
Focus on the future
Good times!
And how you want to feel
Peer pressure!
Not again?
The future…
Come on!

25 July 2006

Don't Tell Me!

A poem?
A song?
Don't tell me!
I don't want to know
Bono
A song about his dad!
I've paid me money
It's my song now!
Don't tell me!

25 July 2006

Life Goes On…

A few years back
Watching *TFI Friday* on telly
A friend said
'Life goes on'
She was having a dig
All my ups and downs
All my fuck-ups
Life goes on…
Regardless

25 July 2006

Testimony

Remember the 2002 ITV drama
The Second Coming with
Christopher Eccleston
And Lesley Sharp? Well
In it, they were looking for
The Third Testament
OK! I am not the second coming, but
My poems are my testimony

And within, explain
'The second coming'
The drama may have been fiction
I believe
My poems to be true
...my Testimony

25 July 2006

In the Town?

If you have read my poems
And you see me in the town...
Don't expect anything!
I have a vision
Hopefully I have passed it on?
There is no more!
Save yourself
Read your Bible...

25 July 2006

The Third Word?

It has just dawned on me
The Bible is two books
The Old Testament
The New Testament
Does that make my poems
The Third Word?
I still believe
There will be somebody
A thousand years from now...

27 July 2006

Brother Lee Love

Brother Lee Love
The priest with the big hands in

The Kenny Everett TV show
What was he pointing at?
1,170 poems
If you still don't know?
Well…

27 July 2006

'Love'

Young girls
Young women
Don't be in a rush
'Love'
It's worth the wait

27 July 2006

Fresh Start

Six, seven years into
The Third Millennium
Still fighting and killing
Fuck the politics!
Your life is worth more than politics???????????
Fresh start?
Lay down thy guns!
If not now?
When!!!!!!!!!!!!!!!!!

28 July 2006

Face

So many wars continue because
They don't wish to lose face
Well?
How much face to gain

Stopping the war
Just?
Stop!!!!!!!!!!!

28 July 2006

The Valley

Living in the valley
Always looking to the horizon
Those girls…
The party?
Always over the hill
Living in town!
The valley wasn't that bad
Green grass?

28 July 2006

This Week

This week on the telly
The BBC news
A war in central Africa
Killed and killing more than in the Second World War
How many wars are there?
Who decides?
What makes the news
So much blood
Fuck?
Life…
Is it worth it?
The bigger picture…
Why?

28 July 2006

Proving Your Point

The biggest gun?
A fast car?
The loudest hi-fi…?
When you don't find the need to
Prove your point!
Not because you are the best
But?
Something inside
That's when you're
Proving your point!!!!!!!

29 July 2006

Wake Up Call!

If you have been reading my poems
This is your…
Wake up call!!!!!!!!!!!
It's your planet
Your life!!!!!!!!!
Sort it out!

31 July 2006

Innuendo

For years I have been
Laughing and joking about sex
The meds can confuse the 'communications'
Then a couple of years back
It came to me!
Life is sex
These days…
I'm a bit more chilled out

31 July 2006

Held Back?

I believe many are held back
Never to be somebody!
I was held back in the 1980s
In hindsight I needed to be held back
If you believe you're held back?
Ask yourself…
Who's holding you back?
And what from
I was a skyrocket in the eighties
If you believe that you are held back
Ask yourself…
Why and what from?

31 July 2006

Am I Done?

If you have been looking through my poems
And you think, yes, OK
But it was just some words…
Then I have failed
The Holy Spirit
Jesus if you like
Is real and moves among us
OK then?
It may not be Jesus
But you cannot say there is nothing
I have tried
In my way
To connect you…
Am I done?

31 July 2006

A Couple of Wishes

One: to be successful with my poems
Two: one day to be successfully off the meds
I believe I am over the nervous breakdowns, but
I am left with this side affect
Oral facial tardive dyskinesia
My tongue involuntary moves around my mouth
It can be sore
Also it drives me up the wall
It's a side affect of twenty-five years of meds
Which happens
When I'm not on the meds
They do say
It will come and go
Will I ever get my second wish?
A couple of wishes…

31 July 2006

Queuing Up for Heaven

Tonight in Pastor Pavitt's church
I was talking with one of the preachers
Pastor had mentioned 'the second coming'
And again how great 'heaven' is
I was thinking, 'Open your eyes'
This is heaven…
I said to the preacher
'A river, a tree
The wind and the rain'
He said
'Yes, some things are beautiful'
Beautiful?
He didn't get it
You are the tree!
You are the wind and the rain!

Creation…
I'm not queuing up for heaven
I'm already there…

2 August 2006

The Big Sleep?

I have looked for 'heaven'
And where it may be…
The idea
The psyche
For myself I don't feel it is in the Bible
But
If you believe
Who is to say you will not get it?
For me?
It may very well be
The big sleep…

2 August 2006

No More TOTP

Last Sunday!
No more *TOTP*
Top of the Pops…
Did 'Pops' stand for popular?
Or
Popping one's balloon?
Perhaps?
No more balloons to pop
For now…

2 August 2006

Private

Yes, I hope some of my ideas and poems
Are successful one day…

But, I do believe one's beliefs
Are private
It's when you try to put your beliefs on another
You can get trouble…
I don't wish to push my poems on anyone
If and when you do read them
It's private…

3 August 2006

Blind

When I say…
The second coming has already happened, and
It's the enlightenment!
Yes!
We have the enlightenment?
Life, planet earth, everything…
But so many are 'blind'
Has to what they actually have.
How many young men will never have to take up arms?
This is not an accident
This is the twenty-first century
Pastor Pavitt's church
They cannot see what's in front of them!
My next door neighbour
With her three kids
She doesn't need a Bible
Smell the flowers
Touch the wind…
I see it everyday
How long must you wait?
Don't be blind!

3 August 2006

The Red Button

That Button!
Is it red?

Anyhow
It's not down to the likes of you and me
And Pastor Pavitt!
I hope to have many a year yet!!!!!!!
Rich or poor…

3 August 2006

No More

No more words
No more poems
I could write and write…
The subject is never-ending
Life…
Yours and mine
That's it
No more!!!!!!!!!

4 August 2006

How Much Blood?

Read my poems, yes!
Tell me I was not on the cross
Crucified!
A million needles…
See the holes in my hands
A million poems…

4 August n2006

Sleep?

If I have all this stuff in my head
How can I sleep?
In the 1980s
I was sedated.
These days

I have accepted my beliefs
And sleep like a baby…

4 August 2006

Good Morning!

If you are reading this
It means my poems are history
The Dawn of the New Tomorrow!
Good morning…

4 August 2006

Nan and Pop. I love you always

Hope and Anchor, Islington N1

Buskin'

Printed in the United Kingdom
by Lightning Source UK Ltd.
130581UK00001B/228/A

9 781847 480965